THE
NEGOTIATION

PHRASE BOOK

The
Words You Should Say
to Get
What You Want

THE

NEGOTIATION

PHRASE BOOK

ANGELIQUE PINET

Avon, Massachusetts

Published by
Adams Media, a division of F+W Media, Inc.
57 Littlefield Street, Avon, MA 02322. U.S.A.
www.adamsmedia.com

Contains material adapted and abridged from *The Everything® Negotiating Book* by Angelique Pinet, copyright © 2005 by F+W Media, Inc.; ISBN 10: 1-59337-152-7, ISBN 13: 978-1-59337-152-4.

ISBN 10: 1-4405-2863-2
ISBN 13: 978-1-4405-2863-7
eISBN 10: 1-4405-3017-3
eISBN 13: 978-1-4405-3017-3

Printed in the United States of America.

10 9 8 7 6 5 4 3 2 1

Library of Congress Cataloging-in-Publication Data
is available from the publisher.

This publication is designed to provide accurate and authoritative information with regard to the subject matter covered. It is sold with the understanding that the publisher is not engaged in rendering legal, accounting, or other professional advice. If legal advice or other expert assistance is required, the services of a competent professional person should be sought.

—From a *Declaration of Principles* jointly adopted by a Committee of the American Bar Association and a Committee of Publishers and Associations

Many of the designations used by manufacturers and sellers to distinguish their product are claimed as trademarks. Where those designations appear in this book and Adams Media was aware of a trademark claim, the designations have been printed with initial capital letters.

This book is available at quantity discounts for bulk purchases.
For information, please call 1-800-289-0963.

Contents

Part II How to Get the Best Deal

Part III Common Negotiations

Introduction

Believe it or not, you've been negotiating all your life. Remember those days of trading baseball cards with friends and exchanging Mom's turkey sandwich for a more delectable snack? Though you probably didn't realize it at the time, you were practicing the art of negotiation. Negotiating as an adult can feel more complicated and intimidating, and there is often more at stake than a few baseball cards or a lunchtime treat. But adapting those skills you developed early on is a worthy pursuit that will serve you well throughout your life. And now, thanks to the ever-increasing speed in which we communicate in both our social and professional lives, negotiation is more important than ever.

How many times have you felt like you should have gotten a better deal on something but didn't know how to do it? How many times have you had the feeling that you paid too much for something because you had no other choice? If you're like most people, you've been there and done that more than you'd like to admit.

If you cringe at the very thought of having to negotiate, you are not alone. You probably envision long hours of haggling with an unpleasant salesperson and getting nowhere in the process or getting stuck on a seemingly endless exchange of e-mails, only to find you haven't made progress until your sixth reply. True, negotiating can be exhausting at times, but for the most part it isn't as dreadful as you might think.

In fact, you negotiate all the time successfully! From accepting a job offer to participating in work-related meetings to hashing out the details of a child's curfew, you've been putting your skills to the test all along. As a consumer, you negotiate your budget on a regular basis to determine what you want versus what you can afford. As a homeowner, you negotiate with many people, like pest exterminators and landscapers. As a spouse, you negotiate sharing household responsibilities and tasks.

Practicing the art of negotiating teaches you how to present your case to others in a way that helps them understand your side of things. You learn how to gain a good amount of control in situations instead of leaving yourself vulnerable. More importantly, you learn that it's okay to ask for the things you want. If you're going to spend a large amount of money on something—a laptop computer, for example—it's not out of line to ask the salesperson to throw a carrying case in with the deal. At worst, she'll say no. At best, you'll be walking out of the store with the computer you wanted and a bag to carry it home in.

Like any game, once you learn the fundamental skills required to play and figure out what you're up against, you can relax and have fun. One of the basic skills of negotiating is learning how to study your opponent. Figuring out how to read body language and facial expressions is a skill you can use anywhere. After all, we interact with people every day, and it's a lot easier to do that when we can understand how they communicate and what they are trying to say. The tips in this book will help you fend off the forceful salesperson and hold your own against a pushy coworker. You'll also gain insight into your own character so you can find your weakest spots and guard against them.

Not only will this book take you through a variety of possible negotiation scenarios, it will also give you the language you need to get the job done. Look for the key negotiation words and phrases (set in bold type and listed at the end of each chapter) that you can keep in the back of your mind and use when negotiating. As you'll learn, what you say and when you say it, as well as the language used in e-mails and contracts, is of utmost importance when negotiating.

As you begin your journey, forget everything you thought you knew about negotiating, and open your mind to all the wonderful things the process has to offer. Once you have a look around, you'll realize how gratifying it is to possess the skills necessary for success. Let this book be your guide into that fascinating world, and discover the many ways you can apply what you've learned to the various facets of your life.

Part I

Before You Start

Chapter 1

The ABCs of Negotiation

BEFORE WE DIVE INTO the language of negotiation—what to say and when to say it—let's explore the reasons for negotiation and how it works. This chapter covers the basics, from the different scenarios in which you might need to negotiate and the players involved to how to set goals and the importance of timing. We'll also discuss alternative methods of striking a deal, for those cases in which negotiation is not the best course of action.

Why Negotiate?

There are endless reasons why negotiations can be beneficial, and most of them have their roots deeply planted in the soil of our bartering ancestor's backyard. Aside from the reasons why negotiations are used in the business world (to increase profit, form large corporations by merging small businesses, and build reputations), the successes you can achieve on a smaller scale in your personal life carry just as much weight as those achieved by companies around the world.

You practice the art of negotiation every day—with your credit card, utility, and car insurance companies, as well as with family, friends, and coworkers. If you think you might be a little late with your water bill payment because it happens to fall on the same day you're having surgery, then you might call the utility company to request an extension. If you're a responsible driver who has never been in an accident or received a speeding ticket, you might ask your car insurance company if they can lower your monthly premium. In both situations, you're asking the company you regularly do business with for a **concession**. What you offer in return is your continued business and a positive opinion about the company's devoted services.

CONCESSION: The act of yielding to another person by giving him a privilege that you don't usually give to other people. For example, during a business meeting, an executive asks for a 10-percent cut in production costs. The other executive agrees to this concession, but she asks for one of her own in return—that products be delivered a month earlier than usual.

In effect, **if two or more people have goals they can help each other reach, they enter into a negotiation**. Carpooling allows drivers to conserve gas mileage, limit the amount of wear and tear on their vehicles, and save on the cost of gas. Babysitting usually requires a teenager to forfeit her Saturday night, but it also gives her spending money for next weekend.

▶ Negotiating for Business

There are men and women all over the world whose professional expertise is in the art of negotiating. Bridges are built, roads are repaired, high-rises are erected, public transportation is rerouted, and streets are named—and all the while, there's a group of professionals negotiating the details of these projects by presenting their ideas and strategies to the appropriate board of directors. Every city within every state vies for a piece of the budget, and the way to get it begins with a group of people who are trained to negotiate. Though most careers involve some negotiating aspects, here are a few professions that will really put your skills to the test:

- Lawyer
- Mediator
- Politician
- Business planner
- Editor
- CEO
- Buyer

If you're not sure you have what it takes to be a great negotiator, study this book, and then try putting your newly acquired skills to use. You can start small at first, for example by negotiating the use of one of your company's conference rooms at a certain time and day (even if it's just to throw someone a surprise birthday party). Then, as you start to feel more confident, you can tackle more complicated situations, like renegotiating your salary and benefits. To hone your negotiating skills even further, you can also attend one of the seminars or workshops available through the websites listed in Appendix C.

▶ **Negotiating for Personal Reasons**

Those creatures of the business world aren't the only ones nego-tiating for a living. If you're a parent, you probably have memories of all the wonderful ways your children have tried to get you to give them what they want. And you can probably recall all the deals you made with them in order to get them to clean their rooms or eat their dinner. While making deals with your children is a great way to get them to do what you ask of them, too much deal-making can have an adverse effect. They start expecting you to always offer a reward in return for something they should be doing as part of their daily chores or personal responsibilities.

In addition to negotiating with children, you probably have to come to an agreement with other members of your family on a regu-lar basis. This might include discussions of division of labor with your spouse, or deciding how your estate will split your family heir-looms among your siblings. Not only are these worthwhile and often necessary negotiations, they're also great opportunities to practice your negotiating skills for use in other arenas. If you can come to an agreement with your spouse about who gets to hold the remote, you can certainly approach your boss about that promotion you've been hoping for. Even encounters with salespeople, waiters, and hosts are great opportunities to see how you do in basic negotiations.

Know Yourself and Your Goals

The first thing you should do before you begin your research is **figure out what you want**. Organizing your thoughts will give you direction and purpose, and the true focus of your plan will come into view. You should never walk into a negotiation unsure of what you're doing there or not quite decided on what you hope to achieve. The other party, potentially a seasoned negotiator, will use this to his advantage by taking a dominant standpoint and mak-ing the purpose of the meeting all about his needs. Additionally, because you're unsure about what's important to you, you'll have nothing to arm yourself with when he hurls a deluge of concessions at you.

To figure out exactly what your goals are, begin by asking your-self the following questions:

- What do I hope to achieve?
- Why are these achievements important to me?
- What is my main goal?
- What are my secondary goals?
- What steps do I need to take to be successful?
- What can prevent me from being successful?
- What am I prepared to do to overcome the obstacles?

List all the goals you hope to achieve, even if some are direct results of others. Next, identify your main goal. Write it out simply and clearly, as it is the primary reason for the strategy you will develop. Bringing your goals to the forefront is only the first step in the process of understanding your objectives. **Prioritizing** goals and devising a plan for reaching them will give you a deeper understanding of what you need to accomplish during the negotiation.

PRIORITIZE: To prioritize is to put in order of importance. Never enter into a negotiation before you've prioritized your goals. If you want to buy a car because you need a way to get to work every morning, your main goal is to buy a reliable vehicle. Secondary goals include whether you want a new or used automobile; whether you prefer a truck, an SUV, or a sedan; and what color you prefer, the features you're looking for, and so on.

▶ **Consider Possible Concessions**

As you're defining goals, keep in mind that **the ability to be flexible may serve you well** at some point during the negotiation. While you don't want to easily give up any of your goals, you do want to keep an open mind about how you can adjust them if it means a mutual agreement can be reached.

As mentioned earlier, concessions are privileges—tiny pieces of gold that need to be rationed wisely. Throughout the course of every negotiation, both parties will ask for one concession in exchange for another. Each party wants to walk out of the room feeling satisfied with the concessions that were agreed upon. If you did your homework—researched, prepared, practiced, and weighed alternatives—you should have a good idea of what concessions you're comfortable making.

When you make concessions during negotiations, here are some guidelines to keep in mind:

- **Know how to present concessions**, from least to most important. Getting the easy ones out of the way first allows you to direct the bulk of your time and energy to more important ones.

- **Exhibit the same amount of resistance for every concession** so the other party can't tell which concessions have more value to you than others. You never want the other party to feel like you've gotten more out of her than she's gotten out of you. If she does, she's likely to ask for a lot more concessions.
- **For every concession you make, ask for one in return.** For example, "I'll give you a discount if you make a higher down payment."
- **Provide reasons for your concessions** so the other party can understand where you're coming from. For example, "I'd like a discount on the sticker price to be able to afford the monthly payments." You'll earn the other party's respect if you prove you're not asking for something just to see if you can get it.

Some experts believe you should always make the first concession. That way you retain control over the ones that are important to you. But others feel that letting the other party make the first concession allows you to take the prize if they overbid. Eventually, you'll develop your own style of negotiating, but for now **go with what feels most comfortable to you**.

▶ Know Your Limitations

Everyone has limits—and you should, too. Knowing yours before you enter into a negotiation helps you stay focused on what's important and allows you to determine whether the agreement is acceptable. The course of a negotiation often changes, and new concessions and limitations have to be established. When this happens, you'll need to determine if your old limitations still apply.

So what kinds of limits should you set? Like goals, **limits should be flexible but steadfast**. Think of them as your bodyguards, ready to protect you on a dime. As soon as you start feeling uncomfortable and things aren't going your way, call attention to your bodyguards so the other party knows they're about to lose your business.

In order to set limits, you should first examine your alternatives. If you could walk away from a negotiation and still have several opportunities waiting, you can be pretty liberal with what limits you set. That's why it can't be stressed enough: **Be sure to have other alternatives before you enter into a negotiation**. It's also good to know what alternatives the other party has lined up since this will determine the importance they place on their concessions.

Know Your Opponent

Your underlying strategy should be largely based on your negotiating opponent. Study your opponent's playing style, and learn as much as possible about why she's investing her time in the negotiation. By reviewing the other party's training, accomplishments, education, and work history, for example, you can better predict what her actions will be and therefore be more prepared to address them.

Try to get the specifics of what the other party's goals are so you can weigh your **leverage** against theirs and adjust your game plan if you need to. It's also a good idea to use the first few minutes of the meeting to discuss some of the objectives you share and those that you do not.

LEVERAGE: Leverage is one party's advantage or ability to overpower the other. In a negotiation, it's important not to let the other party know what your weaknesses are, as these can give them leverage over you. For example, if a potential buyer knows you're selling your car because you need the money, he might try to low-ball you on the price.

▶ **Distinguish Needs and Wants**

A good way to get to know your opponent is to distinguish between their needs and wants. This will allow you to make better decisions about how much time you'll spend discussing particular issues. It will also help you determine what concessions you're willing to make and how flexible you'll be when making them.

One way to separate needs from wants is to explore how many possible outcomes there are per subject. Because needs are more complex and sometimes contingent on other things, they produce the most satisfactory outcomes. Wants, on the other hand, are usually specific requests that cannot be satisfied in more than a few ways. They're usually things like free warranties, an extra shipment of goods, extended services, or some other kind of perk.

If the other party hasn't been upfront about his needs and wants, ask questions to get that information for yourself. Do some creative thinking by providing examples of benefits that might be possible if you had enough information to go on. You could say, "If your biggest concern is price, we can knock off 5 percent here and pick it up on the shipping end. But if you're more concerned with the deadline, then we can get the products to you thirty days early and charge full price." Pay attention to what is most interesting, and come up with more solutions to that problem.

▶ It's a Question of Authority

When you prepare to deal with your opponent, consider how much leeway he has to make concessions and compromise. Is this person really authorized to make decisions, or is he merely a proxy for his manager and unable to make decisions on his own?

Whether you're negotiating with one person or five people, directly ask the participants one by one if they are authorized to negotiate with you and to make and agree to concessions. If you're negotiating with only one person and the answer is no, you will have saved yourself hours of wasted time by asking this important question up front. As soon as the other party reveals he is not authorized to make any deals with you, ask if it would be possible to meet with the person who is authorized to negotiate.

▶ **A Background Check**

Learn as much as you can about the other party's background. One of the most effective ways is to learn about how successful (or unsuccessful) he's been in other negotiations. Talk to anyone you know who's had business dealings with him and ask what his style is and how the negotiations progressed in that person's experience.

Simply asking the other party a few open-ended questions before negotiations is another way to get an idea of whom you're dealing with. Though you can't assume the answers you receive will be 100-percent accurate, asking questions like the following can indicate, to some extent, where the other person is coming from.

- How long have you been with the company?
- How long have you been in your current position?
- What do you hope to gain from this negotiation?

If the other party has been with the company for only three months, then she may be eager to prove herself to her superiors and try to exhibit an aggressive attitude. On the other hand, if the person you're negotiating with has held her position with the company for over fifteen years, she's bound to have a few tricks up her sleeve.

Common and Conflicting Objectives

If you enter into a negotiation with the right mindset, you'll indeed be thinking of ways to make the deal work for both you and the other party. This way of thinking not only builds positive relationships with the people you're working with, but it almost guarantees everyone will be walking away from the table smiling. Before any concessions are made, discuss what objectives you both share and analyze the specific details of the steps that need to be taken to reach those objectives. **Brainstorm other solutions that neither one of you had thought of on your own.** By focusing on the objectives you both have in common, you're streamlining your combined resources to reach a positive outcome.

Once you've settled the objectives you and the other party have in common, talk about the different objectives you have. Something you deem extremely valuable might be something the other person doesn't consider quite so precious; therefore, he has no problem agreeing to make it work for you. Likewise, the concessions you regard as inconsequential are an important part of the other party's agenda and will not hurt you to give up. Allowing each other to have gains that don't require painful losses on either side is an essential part of the game that should never be overlooked.

Analyze the Alternatives

Having one or several alternative courses of action is key to having an advantage. You need to be aware that if the negotiation doesn't work out with the current party, you can turn to others. Alternatives provide you with the confidence to reject offers and to walk away from the negotiation if you're not happy with the way it's going. This is where your power comes from, so use it when you need it the most.

For example, imagine that there's only one car dealership in your town, and you need to buy a car. Think about how disappointed and dejected you would feel if your negotiations with the car dealer did not go at all the way you had hoped. The dealer would be well aware that his business was your only option, and he would take full advantage of the situation by making you agree to almost all of his concessions without having to agree to any of yours. Similarly, if you were the car dealer, what if the only customer who wanted to purchase a particular car decided to walk out the door? You'd either have to come up with even more concessions to try to get her to come back, or you'd just have to cut your losses.

▶ **Plan B and Beyond**

Whatever you're negotiating, **you need to have at least one Plan B** that's as lucrative as your original plan—or else you won't feel it's worth aspiring to when Plan A fails. Plan B should be carefully cultivated under the guise that it's actually an A Plan. The same amount of research, prodding, and strategizing must be applied so you can spring right back into action if your original plan falls through. The more solid alternatives you have under your belt, the more poise you'll exhibit in front of the other party who, make no mistake about it, will probably sense the air of self-assurance that surrounds you.

▶ **Using Alternatives to Your Advantage**

Unquestionably, the other party will have his own set of alternatives to bring to the table. Discovering what other options your negotiating adversary has lined up allows you to assess the level of confidence he has and to determine how much leverage the both of you have. If he doesn't have any options, or the ones you perceive he does have are weak, then you have the upper hand. Now, you may be tempted to have a lot of fun with this and get every little concession you can out of him. However, be mindful that some day the tables may be turned, and you'll be the one with no or few alternatives.

One way to use your advantages for good is to use them as leverage. If at some point during the negotiation the other party has simply gone too far, mention that you have other options that you're prepared to use if things continue on an unsatisfactory level. One of two things will happen: he'll start meeting more of your demands, or he won't take you seriously, in which case you'll opt out of the negotiation altogether. Either way, you have the tools that allow you to move forward to accomplish the goals you've set out for yourself.

▶ **Best Alternative to a Negotiated Agreement (BATNA)**

In 1981 Roger Fisher and William Ury published their bestselling book *Getting to Yes: Negotiating Agreement Without Giving In*. In this book, they explained the concept of the Best Alternative to a Negotiated Agreement, or BATNA. Since then, this idea has become a standard part of negotiation.

Essentially, BATNA is your way to quantify what happens if the deal falls through. For instance, let's say you're negotiating a deal to sell 100,000 widgets to a company. You investigate and determine that keeping the widgets in your warehouse for another month will cost you $3,000. That means your BATNA is slightly more than three cents per widget. In other words, the lowest possible price you'll accept from the company is a bit over 3 percent per widget, because if they offer you anything less, it's cheaper for you not to do the deal and keep the widgets in your warehouse for another month. (If the company offers you exactly three cents per widget, the deal doesn't financially hurt you, but it doesn't benefit you either, so you'd be well advised to negotiate for a higher price.)

BATNA can get very complicated once you factor in things like your long-term relationship with the company (is it worth taking a small financial loss on a deal to cement a relationship with a company that you expect to have a highly profitable relationship with in the future?), delivery time, warranties, or other variables. But the basic point is to try to reduce your negotiating stance to a concrete matter of dollars and cents and determine at what price the deal is worth doing.

Timing Is Everything

Timing is an incredibly important part of the negotiating process. When you're in the midst of a negotiation, you're in a similar position to that of a quarterback during a football game. On the field, he must wait for the right moment to throw the ball to the right person with the right amount of speed and at the right distance. In a negotiation, you must wait for the right time to offer the right terms to the right person under the right circumstances.

One of the most important things to remember about timing is that all parties involved have their own deadlines. Everyone wants to make sure his issues are being discussed and resolved, so some negotiators might try to manipulate time by causing unnecessary delays or by trying to rush the other party into making a quick decision. These tactics should not be tolerated and must be brought up and discussed as soon as they appear.

▶ When the Time Is Right

The time to negotiate is right when you have a well-thought out plan in place and a list of goals you hope to achieve. Steps you've taken ahead of time should include researching your opponent, figuring out your opponent's wants and needs, preparing to suggest alternatives, knowing what your limits are, and making sure you are aware of any tactics that may be used against you.

Never begin negotiations if you are not prepared or have not done extensive **research** into what will be discussed and the people you will be meeting with. If it helps, do a few practice runs with friends or family or seek the advice of a lawyer (depending on the severity of the situation).

RESEARCH: We're not talking about your high school term paper, but the same rules apply. When preparing for a negotiation, you need to know both your subject and the other party inside and out. Research for a negotiation might include visiting your local library, searching the web, or inquiring about your opponent's past dealings with a friend or colleague.

▶ Have Patience

While you want to be wary of intentional delays, **it is also important to have patience**, and lots of it. During the full course of a negotiation period—which can take hours, days, months, or years, depending on the situation—new concessions, problems, concerns, questions, and ideas will come about, and you will need to have the patience to analyze them thoroughly. Since the purpose of negotiating is to come to an agreement that both parties are satisfied with, give the other party (and yourself) enough time to absorb all of the latest information and to formulate decisions based on the new developments.

Feeling tired or weak? Take a break. Walk out of the room and step outside into the fresh air. Drink something cold and grab a snack to restore your energy. By giving your brain the opportunity to recharge, you can walk back into the meeting room feeling alert and ready to continue the discussion.

Key Negotiation Terms in This Chapter
- Concession
- Prioritize
- Leverage
- Research

Key Phrases in This Chapter
- If two or more people have goals they can help each other reach, they enter into a negotiation.
- Figure out what you want.
- List all the goals you hope to achieve.
- The ability to be flexible may serve you well.
- Know how to present concessions, from least to most important.
- Exhibit the same amount of resistance for every concession.
- For every concession you make, ask for one in return.
- Provide reasons for your concessions.
- Go with what feels most comfortable to you.
- Limits should be flexible but steadfast.

- Be sure to have other alternatives before you enter into a negotiation.
- Learn as much as you can about the other party's background.
- Brainstorm to develop other solutions that neither one of you had thought of on your own.
- You need to have at least one Plan B.
- Timing is an incredibly important part of the negotiating process.
- It is also important to have patience.

Chapter 2

A World of
Possibilities

IN EVEN THE SIMPLEST negotiation, there are several variables at play. There's the person or people you're negotiating with, who come with their own communication styles and goals. There's what's at stake: It could be money, or it could be control of the TV for a night. And there's the schedule: You might want to come to a resolution quickly, while the other person feels that he has all the time in the world to negotiate you down. This chapter will help you prepare for a number of possibilities.

Business or Pleasure?

As mentioned in Chapter 1, most of the negotiations you enter into will be either for business purposes or part of your personal life. While one is no more important than the other, they generally need to be handled in different ways. For example, when negotiating with your kids, you can't speak to them the way you would your boss. And vice versa: Your best friend might feel put off if you approach him in an unfamiliar, professional manner. Before you enter into any negotiation, make sure you've considered the arena you're playing in and which communication methods will be most effective with the other party.

▶ Negotiating at Work

At its core, work is just a bunch of people putting their efforts toward a common goal. However, you're expected to act in the professional realm in ways you might not act in the privacy of your home. For example, you may not be able to speak as freely at work as you might with your parents or your spouse. That's okay; it just means you need to prepare for any work negotiations ahead of time so that you don't say something that could be misinterpreted or considered unprofessional. Here are a few examples of how professional language differs from more relaxed, familiar language:

PROFESSIONAL	FAMILIAR
In **exchange** for a 20-percent discount on our order, we promise to do all our business with you for the next fiscal year.	If you clean the bathroom today, I'll do the laundry tomorrow morning.
I haven't been entirely satisfied with the telephone service I've received in the last three months.	I'm not very happy with your grades this semester.
Perhaps we should take a recess and reconvene when we've had time to brainstorm some new ideas.	It's late and we're both tired. Let's finish talking about this in the morning.

EXCHANGE: Any negotiation is an exchange: You're offering to give up something in order to get something else in return. You might be exchanging goods or money or even time. In any case, both parties are trying to get what they want in a way that also satisfies the other.

You want the other party to take you seriously in any sort of negotiation, but this is especially true in business. If the other party doesn't trust that you will stand by your guarantee, they may be hesitant to make a deal with you. While personal matters can be discussed on several occasions over a period time, business is often a one-shot deal. If you don't say what your customer wants to hear while he's in your shop, he might just walk out the door and never come back.

▶ **Negotiating at Home**

If you think that negotiating with friends and family would be easier than negotiating in a professional setting, think again. Just because you're not discussing the financial state of your company or the terms of a business agreement doesn't mean there isn't a lot at stake. When setting boundaries for your kids, for example, they need to know you're serious or they might try to find a way around your rules. When hiring a nanny, you want to make sure that both her needs and the needs of your family are being met.

While you can usually use more relaxed, familiar language when negotiating within your personal life, it's still important that you be firm and clear about what you want. At the same time, **it's important that you hear the other person's side** and make sure that they're getting what they need and want from the deal as well. Here are a few examples of dos and don'ts for negotiating at home:

WHAT TO SAY	WHAT NOT TO SAY
I think nine o'clock is a reasonable bedtime for someone your age. What do you think?	When do you want to go to bed?
Tuesdays and Thursdays are the days when I can most easily pick up the kids from practice. Can you do Mondays and Wednesdays?	I'm really busy and don't have time to pick up the kids. Can you do it?

If at any point you find yourself at an **impasse**, try to put yourself in the other person's shoes for a moment. Also remember that kids and adults communicate and respond in different ways, and therefore you might have to take a different approach if your first attempt doesn't work.

IMPASSE: In a negotiation, an impasse is like a dead end. You've each presented your side of things, but no one is budging enough to reach an agreement. Don't worry; there is a way out. Better than treating impasse like a dead-end is to treat it like a cul-de-sac. Turn around, get back to where you started, and then try a new approach.

Location, Location, Location

We've just discussed *how* to go about negotiating at work and at home. Now it's time to discuss *where* to do it. The place where you choose to conduct negotiations is more important than you might think. **Choose a location where you feel comfortable** meeting the other party and discussing all the details, with plenty of privacy if necessary. Consider the noise level and potential distraction. And don't forget that the space should be appropriate for the type of meeting you have in mind. You might want food served at the meeting or require access to the Internet.

▶ The Home-Field Advantage

Ask anyone who's ever played a sport if their team was more likely to win a game when playing on their home turf, and you'll get a resounding "yes" almost every time. Playing on your turf has many advantages and very few disadvantages. When you're in your own home or office, you have everything you need in close proximity to you. You know where all your important documents, notes, phone numbers, and contacts are, and you can easily find any piece of paper you randomly jotted bits of information on from your last phone call.

The major disadvantage to negotiating on your turf is that you can't just walk out if things are absolutely not going your way and there's no hope that they'll change anytime soon. In that situation, the only thing left to do is explain that you'll need more time to think things through because none of your **objectives** are being met. At this point, the other party will either ask you what needs to happen for the negotiation to continue, or she'll walk out the door and hopefully mull over what went wrong and contact you later on.

OBJECTIVE: An objective is a purpose or goal, the thing you came to a negotiation to accomplish. While your objectives should be flexible, it's important to have a clear idea of which objectives you're willing to compromise on and which you're not.

▶ **An Away Game**

There are some people who feel just as comfortable on the other party's turf as they do on their own. The key to having this kind of confidence is to always come prepared. Try using the STOP technique (before you leave your home or office) each time you have to be the visiting team:

- **Stock** your bag or briefcase with any supplies you might need. Though the place where you're going probably already has supplies, they won't have the specific things you like to use. For example, pack your favorite pen or highlighter, the calculator you feel most comfortable using, your business cards, and anything else you keep handy in your own space.

- **Take** everything with you. When in doubt, take it along. It's better to have too much of everything than not enough of the right thing. You never know what you might need, so it won't hurt to take along notes, forms, contact information for people you might need to get in touch with, and so on. If these items are all accessible on your laptop, then all the better.

- **Organize** your briefcase. Keep important documents separate from miscellaneous documents, papers that are for your eyes only separate from those that you'll be sharing with the other party, and information not related to the meeting separate from information that is. Staying organized does wonders for the image you present to the other party. And, the more together you are, the more confident you'll feel.

- **Prepare** for anything. Let's say one of your alternative negotiators has an office not too far from where you'll be negotiating with the current party. It's not a bad idea to prepare for a meeting with them in case things don't go well with this negotiation. You'll already have your materials by your side and you'll still be in the mindset to do business.

Personalities at Play

People's negotiating styles are dependent on their personalities. Understanding your own personality and how it drives you will help you figure out your own negotiating style. It will also help you identify what kind of negotiator your counterpart is. Since part of successful negotiating involves knowing as much as you can about your counterpart, these clues are invaluable. They allow you to assess and predict the other party's behavior throughout the negotiation.

▶ Aggressive and Dominant

You can identify an aggressive negotiator from the following personality traits:

- Demanding
- Self-centered
- Controlling
- Defensive
- Competitive
- Forceful
- Rude
- Intimidating
- Ambitious
- Impatient

These negotiators act fast and don't want to spend any more time with you than necessary. Before meeting with them, have all the facts prepared, and be ready for a speedy discussion. They have no patience and will try to rush you along every chance they get.

Their strategy involves **withholding** any information they think you might benefit from, inflating and deflating numbers, and embellishing or leaving out facts. They often throw temper tantrums and like to use the bottom-line technique because they always want to keep things moving quickly.

WITHHOLD: To withhold is to refrain from giving or granting. This can have both positive and negative connotations in a negotiation. A person who withholds might just be standing his ground to prevent getting taken advantage of, or he might be trying to force his opponent to settle for less than they deserve.

Handle these negotiators with care and know that they are always just seconds away from exploding into a fit of anger. They're not the type of people to hold back, and they're certainly not about to let you have any control over the discussion.

▶ Passive and Submissive

This personality is the exact opposite of the aggressive personality. Submissive negotiators tend to exhibit the following characteristics:

- Nice
- Friendly
- Considerate
- Insecure
- Uncomfortable with conflict
- Sensitive
- Shy
- Calm
- Reserved
- Obedient

If you fall into this category, steer clear of holding any discussions with the aggressive negotiator. Because submissive personalities are more focused on pleasing other people, they get taken advantage of frequently.

Submissive negotiators want others to like them. They'll do whatever they can to make the other party happy, even if it means giving up extra concessions or letting the other party **renege** on one of theirs. Because their main goal is to put the other party first, their secondary goals are usually focused on the other party's issues and how to satisfy them.

RENEGE: To renege is to go back on one's word. This happens all the time in negotiations, which is why you need to protect yourself. When you come to an agreement with the other party, make it official with a contract or some other written statement.

 Logical and Analytical

Analytical people can be recognized by the following traits:

- Probing
- Apprehensive
- Mistrusting
- Thoughtful
- Organized
- Prepared
- Detail-oriented
- Logical
- Firm
- Critical

These negotiators need to have all the facts, details, and information to understand what's taking place at the negotiating table. Instead of rushing ahead, they want to be prepared first. Their main objective is to walk away from the negotiation feeling like they truly accomplished something. In order for them to achieve their goal, they must first be successful in reaching their secondary goals, which involves a careful review of all the available information, a logical approach to the solution, and an explanation of why it all works.

 Friendly and Collaborative

The collaborative negotiator is easy to recognize from the following traits:

- Fair
- Empathetic
- Considerate

- Appreciative
- Honest
- Tactful
- Friendly
- Open-minded
- Resourceful
- Flexible

These are the ideal candidates for handling negotiations because they possess the principles needed to reach **win-win** solutions. They understand that a negotiation is not a battle. Rather, it's a process of attaining mutual successes with the least possible amount of resistance and negativity.

WIN-WIN: This one's pretty self-explanatory, but it's a term that comes up a lot in negotiations. A win-win is a resolution that's advantageous to both sides—in other words, the ideal outcome of any negotiation.

Collaborators are concerned with satisfying everyone's main goals by working toward results that allow them all to walk away from the table in agreement. It's also important to them to build trust and encourage and develop solid relationships that last well into the future. Their secondary goals include learning as much as possible about the other person and his objectives so that the desired outcome can be achieved.

▶ Evasive and Uncooperative

These negotiators can be recognized from the following traits:

- Insecurity
- Carefulness
- Introversion
- Timidity
- Evasiveness
- Reservedness

- Unresponsive
- Cold
- Pessimistic
- Easily embarrassed

It's hard to imagine evasive negotiators at a negotiation because their way of dealing with issues is to disregard them altogether. That's not to say that they don't hope to succeed by walking away with all their needs met; they just don't know how to approach the issues, so they don't approach them at all. Evasive negotiators usually oscillate between what to do and what not to do because they're so afraid of making the wrong move and being crushed by the opposing party.

One of the major goals of these negotiators is to endure the negotiation and to try not to lose. The reason for this struggle could be insecurity, lack of knowledge about the subject, or anything else that may make them feel too uncomfortable to participate. Throughout it all, their only survival technique is to avoid saying anything that might cause a disagreement or further discussion of the issues.

▶ Expressive and Communicative

Expressive negotiators may be any of the following:

- Playful
- Spontaneous
- Energetic
- Talkative
- Sociable
- Self-involved
- Easily distracted
- Enthusiastic
- Extrovert
- Ambitious

These negotiators are generally very animated and always portray a fun-loving attitude. It's important to build rapport with them at the beginning of the negotiation because it makes them more comfortable when they know people are enjoying their company. It also allows them to work their "magic" on you by completely winning you over with their charm.

Aside from becoming your new best friend, the main goal of expressive negotiators is to see how much they can get out of the deal by using their social skills and optimism. When you reject one of their offers, they tend to take it personally. They fail to understand how the discussion could be about anything other than them. They spent a lot of time hamming it up with you, and they expect to be rewarded!

Deadlines and Delays

Our lives would be so much easier without the **pressure** of deadlines. We could work at a relaxed pace and forego late nights at the office forever. Isn't that a nice thought? Now think about what life would be like without the help of deadlines: the warehouse that ships your products to your customers only does so once every three weeks; your mechanic gets around to fixing your car whenever the mood strikes him. While deadlines can make life complicated, they also help us get things done.

PRESSURE: At any point in a negotiation, one or both parties may use pressure, or the exertion of force, as a tactic. They may do this by declaring a deadline or threatening consequences, such as losing the deal altogether. Applying pressure is a legitimate power play in a negotiation, but it should always be done carefully and respectfully.

▶ Real or Imaginary?

On a day-to-day basis, you encounter very real deadlines—like those at work, at your children's school, or within your budget. These deadlines are clearly defined and easy to recognize. But how do you tell if a deadline proposed by the other negotiating party is real? One approach is to use a formula that combines what you already know about your counterpart with what you can assess from his delivery of the transaction. If, throughout the course of your research, you discovered the other party has a history of using unfair tactics, employing an intimidating style of negotiating, and being hard to work with, re-examine how he conveyed the deadline information to you. If he was demanding, you can almost be sure his deadline is imaginary.

To test if your assumption is accurate, ask your counterpart a series of questions. His responses will not only answer the questions you asked him, they will also answer the questions you're asking yourself:

- "Why is this deadline necessary?" answers your internal question, "Is this a real deadline?"
- "Is this deadline the best option?" answers your internal question, "How does the other party benefit from this deadline?"
- "What are the consequences if I don't accept this deadline?" answers your internal question, "What do I stand to lose if I refuse to comply?"

If the answers you receive do not justify the need for a deadline, then ask for an extension. Just like anything else, **deadlines are negotiable**. They should not be used as a means of pressuring you to make decisions in haste. If the other party still will not budge, put the focus on objectives. This way, the issue can transition into something more goal-oriented.

▶ The Value of Limitations

Though it's more common for deadlines to be used against you, there are ways to have them work in your favor. One of the most discouraging aspects of a negotiation is feeling like you're getting nowhere. If the other party is stalling and you're ready to move on, circle back to the focus of the discussion by instituting a deadline that causes her to spring back into action. Make it apparent that she's in danger of losing your business if she doesn't give you a decision by a specified time and date, at which point all deals will be off. Remember, work toward both your and the other party's goals, but don't allow her to push you around.

If two of your other alternatives have already made you offers, take advantage of setting a deadline that urges the party you're dealing with now to make an offer before the others expire and you're no longer able to compare all three. Be considerate when presenting the limitation so as not to offend the other person, and just give her the facts: "I hope I can have your offer today because I'm expecting two others this evening."

▶ Waiting It Out

Most concessions are made close to a negotiation's deadline, if there is one. The explanation is simple. The more time the two parties invest in the negotiation process, the less likely they will be to pull out. If one party begins demanding new concessions, the opponents are more likely to give in so that negotiations can come to a successful end. However, sitting tight until the end and then asking for additional concessions is a high-risk strategy, and you will need patience and self-confidence to use it.

Your counterpart is aware of this strategy, and it is quite likely he'll try to use it. When he does, counter the tactic by examining his position:

- What is his motivation?
- Is he trying to buy time, and if so, why?
- What does he hope to achieve?
- What does he stand to lose?
- If I opt out, how does that affect his plan?
- Does he have a hidden **agenda**?

AGENDA: Quite simply, an agenda is a plan. It can be straightforward and obvious, such as a list of the three things you'd like to discuss in a meeting, or it can be a hidden plan that you or your opponent is not revealing for tactical reasons.

Another way to use patience as a tactic—one that's not so chancy—is to acquire more time to conduct additional research. If you have drawn a number of conclusions about your counterpart or speculated why the company he works for is putting pressure on him to close the deal, it's in your best interest to dig a little deeper to test your assumptions. You might be surprised to discover just how important your deal is to them.

The Business of Body Language

Sometimes the most important conversation you can have with another person involves no words at all. Becoming fluent in body language requires a great deal of time, effort, practice, and application, but it's worth the effort. Honing your body language skills will help you uncover hidden agendas, discover a person's true feelings, gain insight into someone's character, predict reactions, and become aware of your own nonverbal behavior.

▶ "Reading" Versus "Speaking"

The challenge of reading body language lies in how misleading it can be. It's not an exact science, and many nonverbal cues can be interpreted in numerous ways. Even though there are some standard generalizations, each signal is unique to the person and the context. Most of the time we don't know our bodies are silently communicating with the rest of the world; even if even we did, we probably wouldn't know what we were saying.

Speaking body language is instinctive. People don't consciously move their arms when they speak—it just happens. It's natural for arms to move, feet to tap, and eyes to turn away when engaged in verbal conversation. In fact, it feels very unnatural to carry out these behaviors consciously. Because it's awkward to make your body go against its own grain, these skills must be learned and developed over time in order to make the act seem effortless.

▶ Common Nonverbal Cues

There are literally thousands of nonverbal cues to discover, not to mention thousands of ways to interpret them—so many that they could fill a book of their own! The following are just some of the most common nonverbal cues and their functions:

BODY LANGUAGE	POSSIBLE MEANING
Crossed arms	Defensive, immovable, opposing
Crossed legs, ankles	Competitive, opposing
Clenched hands, strong grip on object	Frustration
Cocked head	Interested, attentive
Covering mouth with hands	Dishonesty
Fidgeting	Apprehensive, unconfident
Finger tapping or drumming	Boredom
Frequent nodding	Eagerness
Hands on hips	Confidence, impatience
Hands on cheek, chin or glasses	Thinking, examining
Hands on table or desk	Poise
Head in hand	Disinterested, disrespectful
Leaning forward	Enthusiasm
Open arms, hands	Open-minded, approachable
Perpetual eye blinking	Deception
Rubbing nose, forehead	Uptight, confrontational
Side glance	Suspicion
Sitting on edge of seat	Prepared, enthusiastic
Slouching, leaning back	Challenging, rejecting
Throat-clearing	Nervousness

Spend time getting the basics down before you move on to the more complicated cues, such as breathing, which can be tricky to recognize at first due to its subtle nature. Jot down notes about the other party's body language each time an issue is discussed so you can analyze it later if you don't have time to do it on the spot.

▶ Dress for Success

How you choose to dress says a lot about who you are. If you plan on pursuing a career in the business world, you'll need to dress in appropriate business attire. People who respect the game show it by looking the part, and they get more respect for doing so. Would you expect a football player to wear anything on the field other than his team uniform? While not all professions have adopted a standard way of dressing, the business world has, and the reasons are justifiable. Fortunately, there's no need to sacrifice style for a professional look; just follow a few simple rules and you'll be ready for the executive runway in no time.

For men, a good rule of thumb is to stick with dark blue or gray suits. Black is acceptable, but looks a little intense or even morbid; you can offset this with pinstripes. A crisp shirt, complementary tie, and polished, scratch-free dress shoes are also important. For women, the same rules apply, and you have the options of a blouse and a skirted suit to add to your wardrobe. Keep heels at or below two inches, and wear nylons. Soft, muted hues such as beige, taupe, white, or tan work well, but darker colors project more authority.

People who hold reputable positions tend to dress conservatively to project an air of importance, status, and intelligence. This in turn allows the other party to place confidence in the businessperson's abilities to perform their job well. If you hired an accountant to carefully manage your $2.5-million lottery winnings, how would you feel if he greeted you in a ripped T-shirt, khakis, and sandals?

▶ Vocalization

Your voice is instrumental in expressing how you feel. Tone, tempo, and cadence play as crucial a role as word choice in communication. Use your voice to get your point across more effectively, to get someone's attention, to soothe or calm someone who's upset, or to gain insight into your counterpart's intentions.

Tone is comprised of many elements: pitch (high or low frequency), stress (emphasis), and volume (loudness) are the elements you need to monitor. It is used to place importance on certain words, and if not done correctly, your counterpart can totally misread your meaning and emotionality. Consider the following example, where boldface indicates emphasis on a particular word:

- **What** do you want?
- What **do** you want?
- What do **you** want?
- What do you **want**?

Notice how the meaning of each question is changed depending on where the emphasis is? If it's still unclear, read each one out loud with the proper inflection and think about how you would react in each situation.

Loud tones can be used to get someone's attention or to make a point, but they may sound threatening and filled with anger. Soft, quiet tones make people feel relaxed and safe, but they may also signal weakness and be ignored.

Tempo refers to how fast you speak (rushing through sentences or slow and calculated), while cadence is the rhythm or style of your voice (dull monotone or exciting variations). If your counterpart is speaking too fast, he may be nervous or apprehensive about something. If his voice drones on without any use of tone or pitch, he may be uninterested or distracted by something.

Key Words in This Chapter
- Exchange
- Impasse
- Objective
- Withhold
- Renege

- Win-win
- Pressure
- Agenda

Key Phrases in This Chapter
- You want the other party to take you seriously.
- It's important that you hear the other person's side.
- Choose a location where you feel comfortable.
- People's negotiating styles are dependent on their personalities.
- Deadlines are negotiable.
- How you choose to dress says a lot about who you are.

Chapter 3

Avoiding Pitfalls

NEGOTIATING FOR THE FIRST time can be intimidating, and you are bound to make a few mistakes along the way. That's okay; it's part of the learning process. Even the most experienced negotiators consider how they could have done things differently. Like chess, negotiating involves learning the rules, studying different players' styles, and developing your own skills over time. To help you in your learning process, this chapter covers some pitfalls you'd do well to avoid, as well as some key phrases to help you out of tough spots.

Dealing with Difficult People

Everyone has a different outlook on life. Our individual experiences influence how we see the rest of world and how we react to what we encounter. When two or more parties sit down at the negotiating table, each person has a different perspective on the situation and operates directly from that viewpoint. The trick is to find a way to balance all the different personalities involved in the discussion so the focus remains on the subject matter and not on the individuals themselves.

▶ **Reaching an Understanding**

When the person you're working with becomes a problem, the deal-making process can be grueling and unpleasant. It's hard to concentrate on your strategy when you feel like you're walking on eggshells, worrying about how the other person will respond to your next statement, or feeling frustrated because you can't find a way to get along. Deal with this problem early on by acknowledging that you do in fact have a common interest—the objectives that brought you both to the table in the first place. Here are some ways to get the conversation rolling:

- It's clear that we have different working styles, but **the important thing is that we share a common goal**.
- I respect your opinion about this, but I feel differently. **Let's try to reach an agreement that we're both happy with.**
- **Let's talk about how we can both get what we want** without stepping on each other's toes.
- **I'm willing to compromise** on a few issues so that we can close this deal. If you're willing to do the same, I think we can figure out a solution.
- Here's what I hope to achieve from these negotiations. Now tell me what you hope to achieve, and **let's see if we can meet in the middle**.

If the other party refuses to be accommodating, fights you every step of the way, and continues to use **positional negotiating**, examine the behavior by openly discussing it. Let her know how you view the situation, and talk about how your personality differences prevent the two of you from working toward a win-win outcome. For example, you might be frustrated with her quick, defensive reactions to your requests, while she might be impatient with your slow responses.

POSITIONAL NEGOTIATING: This is another way of referring to win-lose negotiating. It means one party is only looking out for his own interests and isn't attempting to reach a win-win solution. This results in one party achieving its goals at the expense of the other party.

By calling attention to these differences, you might discover that she's used to working in a fast-paced environment and handling every situation with speed. She in turn could benefit from learning that your slower approach isn't deliberate; you have a tendency to analyze everything.

Try to understand where the other party is coming from, and be open about where you stand. As long as neither of you places blame or gets upset, you should be able to work things out.

▶ Choose Words Carefully

The English language contains a few seemingly innocent words that can surprise you with how much power they truly hold. Tucked inside a harmless sentence, these words can create a tone that sounds offensive to anyone who already has a defensive personality. Even if you have good intentions, the other party could misunderstand your statement and react negatively to it.

Avoid sounding aggressive by making the following adjustments to your word choices.

- **"I" versus "you"**: Instead of saying, "You still didn't answer my question," rephrase the statement: "I'm sorry, I still don't understand. I think a few examples would give me a better idea." By placing the blame on yourself, the other party doesn't feel like you're criticizing and is more willing to communicate.
- **Negative versus positive**: Words like *can't, won't, shouldn't,* and *don't* should be used sparingly. Instead of saying, "I can't do that" try "I have a few other options I'd like to get your opinion on." It will be easier for you to explain why you can't accept his offer if you present alternative solutions.
- **"But"**: Think of this word as a cutoff point, beyond which your counterpart will stop listening to what you're saying.

For example: "Our production costs are high, but the materials you're requesting are expensive." To the person on the defense, this could sound like you're attacking his original idea by telling him he's wrong to have had it in the first place. Simply remove "but" from the sentence to assure he hears your response: "Production costs are high; the supplier charges X-amount for these materials."

Whenever possible, **use facts to back up your objections** to the other party's request. Providing evidence for your protest shows him you're not trying to be difficult and helps him better understand your position.

The Stress Factor

Stress is a natural part of life. We experience it when we go through difficult life changes, such as losing a job or a loved one, and we experience it on happy occasions, such as when getting married or having a baby. The accompanying sleeplessness, clammy hands, and other reactions to stress are evolutionary leftovers of our ancestors' fight-or-flight response. Stress means that something has changed or escalated and we're trying to figure out how to deal with it.

It makes sense, then, that stress would be a natural part of the negotiation process. When a deadline is approaching or an opponent is demanding that you alter the terms of your proposed agreement, you might feel like you're under the gun or backed into a corner with nowhere to go. When things get to this point, remember that this is a negotiation, not jail time. You're as much in control of the proceedings as the other side is, and you each have the right to be heard.

That said, there are bullies out there. Unforgiving negotiators know that the best way to throw other people off course is to tamper with their inner strengths and expose their weaknesses. In other words, they know exactly what buttons to push to upset you. Your first line of defense against this tactic is to know what your **hot buttons** are. Consider these questions:

- Do you get defensive when your ideas are shot down?
- Do you take it personally when you're verbally attacked?
- Do you get insulted when someone doesn't agree with you?
- Do you get angry when someone rolls his eyes at you?
- Are you easily offended? How so?
- Are you easily intimidated? What are you afraid of?
- How strongly does guilt affect you? Are you quick to give in?

Next, think about how you feel when you're put in similar situations. What emotions do you feel the most? What is your body telling you?

HOT BUTTON: A hot button is a controversial subject or issue that is likely to rouse strong feelings. Some negotiators will press your hot buttons just to agitate you and throw off your focus. Don't fall for this trick. Let it roll off your back and get back to the matter at hand.

It helps to develop a system for dealing with stress. Go into a quiet room alone and close your eyes for five minutes to regain strength. Take a walk around the block to expend any negative energy. Jot down your favorite quote, a passage from your favorite book, or a saying from your favorite philosopher—anything that helps you feel centered—and read it to yourself when you're feeling overwhelmed. If it's music that relaxes you, take a few minutes to listen to your favorite tune.

Managing Concessions

Another common pitfall to guard against is the mismanagement of concessions. In Chapter 1 we discussed when you should make them and when you should ask for them. Here, we'll look at the mistakes that cause you to fall short of important concessions and those that result in your giving up too much. Keep track of the concessions you give and receive; you never know when the tally can be used to influence a decision.

▶ Ask Away

When you sit down to prepare your proposal, you'll have to decide what you think is appropriate and what isn't. From small requests to major ones, write them all down as if you can't live without a single one, and highlight the major ones so that you'll remember them even when the discussion gets intense. As the negotiation proceeds, check each one off your list as you go along so you don't skip over any.

There's no need to feel greedy or afraid to ask for something you think the other party views as trivial. The truth is, you never know what your counterpart will be willing to agree to. You'll regret it later if with **hindsight** you realize that the concessions you didn't ask for were things you could have easily gotten.

HINDSIGHT: Hindsight is the recognition of the realities of a situation after it's happened. Ever heard the expression, "Hindsight is 20/20"? All it means is that often things are clearer when looking at them in the past. There will be times when you look back on negotiations and see places where you went wrong or gave up concessions unnecessarily. Don't beat yourself up. Instead, use them as learning experiences.

▶ Handing It Over

When it's your turn to give up concessions, one of the biggest mistakes you're liable to make is thinking that the other party values what you're offering as much (or as little) as you do. If your strategy is to offer something you think he wants in exchange for something you really want, the danger lies in the assumption that he will view the trade as being equal. If you take this chance and discover that he doesn't think the deal is fair, he may feel like you're trying to take advantage of him and, as a result, begin withholding concessions.

One more thing to remember about making concessions is that you should **always ask for something in return**. Let's say you give something away without making a request for yourself because you figure you can ask for something later. For now, you'd rather move on to a point you've been eager to discuss. Then "later" comes, and the same situation happens again. If you haven't been keeping track of concessions, you'll fail to see how much you've given away compared to how much you've received. Another drawback is that you'll have to backtrack and re-evaluate the issues under discussion at the time you gave up the concession.

Weighing Risks

Negotiating is risky business. Risks can be personal or professional, private or social, financial or emotional, and they're all measured differently from one person to the next. For example, you might have no reservations about asking your coworker to trade shifts with you, but you might be afraid to ask your landlord to replace your dishwasher because you worry she'll accuse you of breaking it. Before entering into any negotiation, it's important to acknowledge all the risks and then measure whether those risks are worth taking.

For example, in a business negotiation you might be worried about your reputation. In this case, consider whether you can withstand the ruthlessness of your counterpart. As you're conducting your research, pay close attention to the details that could put you in over your head financially. Think about how willing you are to put your career on the line and how much you can afford to lose.

On the other hand, if you usually feel intimidated by taking chances that could have an adverse effect on your success, try to build your confidence level. You can start small. For instance, next time you're at the movie theater ordering snacks, ask if you can get a bag of the popcorn that you just saw popping instead of one of the bags that have been sitting on the shelf. Go to a restaurant that's not too busy and ask to sit at a particular table. These small successes will give you the courage to ask for what you want, both in your personal life and at the negotiation table.

One risk you should never feel good about taking is skipping the preparation stage. **Your strength comes from knowledge.** If you know what you're talking about, you'll feel like you're competent enough to get positive results. You'll also be less likely to back down, which puts not only your self-esteem at risk but also the other party's respect for you.

The Closing Stage

The blunders you make during the **closing** stage can seem a little more drastic than the others we've already discussed. At closing, your negotiations are finalized; once the deal is done, there's no looking back. Before you panic, there are a few things you can do to help make sure you don't end up with a resolution you didn't bargain for.

CLOSING: The closing is the final phase of a transaction, resulting in a resolution. The word *phase* is key here. A closing is not like a bad dream you wake up from and realize you did everything wrong. Instead, think of it as a final chance to review the negotiation as a whole and make any last-minute adjustments.

When re-examining the details of the negotiation, you might come across a miscalculation you made or an inaccuracy in one of your concessions. You may even discover a concession that you didn't mean to make. When this happens, bring it up immediately, even if you feel embarrassed. The longer you wait, the more it will seem like you purposely planted the error as part of a ploy.

In addition to having the courage to point out your own mistakes, you'll need to have the courage to stand up to the other party's last-minute tactics. It's never too late to make changes, even at this stage, but you want to keep them to a minimum because this is when you're trying to get the other party to make commitments. If she asks for an extra concession here and an extra one there, don't give in just to be the good guy and help close the deal faster. Don't worry about being liked during this stage. More importantly, don't be afraid to say "no."

Making decisions because you feel pressured to do so is one of the worst mistakes you can make, particularly during the closing. Take all the time you need to put the final stamp on the agreements you made, and you'll feel more confident about your decisions later.

While this slower pace may incur the wrath of your counterpart, don't be coerced into finalizing anything you're not ready for. Additionally, know that most deadlines can be negotiated. Even if the extension is just for a few hours, use the extra time efficiently. Go back to the table early if you're able to work out your issues before time is up.

Key Words in This Chapter
- Positional negotiating
- Hot button
- Hindsight
- Closing

Key Phrases in This Chapter
- The important thing is that we share a common goal.
- Let's try to reach an agreement that we're both happy with.
- Let's talk about how we can both get what we want.
- I'm willing to compromise.
- Let's see if we can meet in the middle.
- Use facts to back up your objections.
- Always ask for something in return.
- Your strength comes from knowledge.

Case Study—Difficult People

Imagine a negotiating session that goes something like this.

Ms. Salesperson: Good afternoon. I'm glad you could make the time to see me. I'm sure you won't regret it.

Mr. Grouchy: Well, I'm not so sure. Frankly, I've got a very busy afternoon and I don't have much time to waste. I'm really not sure there's any point in our speaking. Sorry to speak bluntly, but that's the way I am.

Ms. Salesperson: I certainly understand that your schedule is very compressed. I'll be brief as I can. We've dealt with your company before, and I understand that you've agreed to take delivery of 10,000 units. As I see it what we really need to settle here is the issue of delivery date and warranty.

Mr. Grouchy: Not so fast, not so fast. Who told you we were going to take 10,000 units?

Ms. Salesperson: That's the figure that was given in the deal memo that . . .

Mr. Grouchy: Well, I can tell you right now that we're taking only 5,000 units, and only if you can guarantee delivery by next week. If you can't do a deal along those lines, we might as well stop talking right now.

Ms. Salesperson: I . . .

Mr. Grouchy: There's no point in arguing about it. That's my position, and I'm sticking to it. The only question is if you can meet these terms or not.

Ms. Salesperson: (pausing for a moment) Sir, I'm sorry if there's been a misunderstanding between our two companies. Believe me, I want to do what's best for you as well as for my company. But I think **we should recognize that we're really in this together**. We have a common goal, and we need to work toward it.

Mr. Grouchy: What common goal is that?

Ms. Salesperson: Well, you need these units delivered in a timely fashion, and my company can supply them. We just need to arrive at **a solution that works for both of us**. I think if we're flexible and focus on our mutual benefit we can work something out.

Mr. Grouchy: All right. What are you suggesting?

Ms. Salesperson: Your representative had indicated previously that you were willing to take delivery on 10,000 units, but since you're saying now you only need 5,000 units, I'm assuming something has changed. **Can you tell me what about your needs is different?**

Mr. Grouchy: Things have changed since we talked to your people. We're no longer servicing five out of the twenty stores that are on our list. Those five stores are closing this month, so our needs are less.

Ms. Salesperson: That makes a difference, of course. But you'll need some backup inventory all the same, won't you?

Mr. Grouchy: We can just order that from you when we need it.

Ms. Salesperson: But it will be more expensive to make a series of smaller orders, won't it? Even with the increased warehousing costs of storing surplus inventory? Though I can understand the need to find the right balance between an appropriate inventory and running into shortages that could cause delays in supplying your retailers. Why don't we **meet in the middle** and say 7,500 units?

Mr. Grouchy: Okay, that would probably work, but what about delivery? This whole thing has dragged on too long, and if we can't get delivery by next week I don't think that there's a point in doing a deal for any units because we won't be able to move them into the stores in time.

Ms. Salesperson: When next week is the latest you could take delivery?

Mr. Grouchy: We could move them through the warehouse processing system in a day and a half. If they're going to be in the stores for the weekend and we allow one day for delivery, that means we'd need them in the warehouse by Wednesday noon at the absolute latest.

Ms. Salesperson: **I'll have to speak to my supervisors** to make sure that's possible, but we might be able to manage that. I know it's important to accommodate your delivery schedule. If that tight a turnaround proves difficult for us, are **there some other options** we could examine?

Mr. Grouchy: Well, could we ship directly from your warehouse to the stores? That would save us a day and a half.

Ms. Salesperson: That's an interesting idea. It might raise some process issues, since we don't have the stores programmed into our system, but I can certainly look into that. If we elect to go that route, would you be willing to pay a somewhat higher per unit cost?

Mr. Grouchy: How much are you thinking?

Ms. Salesperson: What about ten cents per unit?

Mr. Grouchy: We could do five cents.

Ms. Salesperson: Let me run some numbers. I think we could get that down to seven cents per unit with a discount on shipments to individual stores that were 1,000 units or above.

Mr. Grouchy: Yes, that would work.

Ms. Salesperson: Great. Regarding the warranty, if we go with the second scenario we'd start the warranty as soon as the products reached the stores rather than when they entered your warehouse, since we'd be bypassing that. Is that okay with you?

Mr. Grouchy: Yes, I guess that would be okay.

Ms. Salesperson: Wonderful. Mr. Grouchy, **I appreciate your time and willingness to work things out to our mutual benefit**.

Mr. Grouchy: Oh, that's fine. Sorry I was a bit harsh with you when we started. There's been a lot of stress around here this week.

Ms. Salesperson: Not at all. I'm glad we could arrive at a tentative agreement. I'll confirm these points with my boss and **give you a call tomorrow morning**. Does 10 A.M. work for you?

Mr. Grouchy: Yes, that'll be fine.

Note the following points about this negotiating session:

1. The salesperson didn't let Mr. Grouchy intimidate her; instead, she used calming, neutral phrases to defuse the situation and turn the discussion to the specifics of the negotiation.
2. The salesperson asked for specifics of the situation, operating from facts rather than emotions and stressing the need to find a mutually satisfactory solution.

3. Neither side in the negotiation gave anything away for free.
    Any concessions were matched by a request for a concession
    from the other side.

4. The salesperson made clear she would have to get an agree-
    ment from her boss to the new terms, and she set a specific
    time for a follow-up conversation with the customer.

Both sides were willing to meet in the middle to find a win-win
solution; neither side showed any interest in positional negotiating,
which would have created a stalemate.

Part II

How to Get the Best Deal

Chapter 4

Negotiator Beware: Common Tricks and Tactics

SLY NEGOTIATORS OFTEN RELY on techniques designed to manipulate and deceive their opponents by toying with their emotions. These maneuvers can take the form of competitive offers, imaginary deadlines, and ultimatums, leaving little room for negotiation. While it's not advisable to use all of the ploys described in this chapter to achieve win-win success, knowing how to recognize them is your best defense against falling for these tricks.

Good Guy/Bad Guy

Probably the most easily recognizable trick is the good guy/bad guy **tactic**, an entertaining display of two people who are on the same team but act out completely opposite roles in an effort to control your emotions with their distortion of reality. If the good guy/bad guy act is successful, the victim of this mind game is rendered powerless.

TACTIC: A tactic is a plan or procedure used to produce a desired outcome. Tactics are the tools of negotiation; you will use them, and so will your opponent. The key is not to be fooled by any tactics intended to throw off your focus or force you into making concessions you hadn't planned on.

Here's how the technique works. The bad guy is the disagreeable negotiator, always unreasonable, irritable, and angry. The good guy, on the other hand, is calm and helpful, the peacemaker who interjects to tell the bad guy to ease up a little bit. This good guy/bad guy routine is set up to make you feel like the good guy is on your side and will do whatever he can to help you.

Surely you've viewed this scene on a TV show or in a movie. The bad cop interrogates the murder suspect by screaming, threatening, and bullying him, then storms out of the interrogation room only to be replaced by the good cop who befriends the suspect by offering him cigarettes, being nice to him, and promising to help him out of the situation he's in if he just reveals where the murder weapon is or where the body is buried.

Another place you might have witnessed this scenario is at the car dealership. The salesperson will play the good guy and his manager, who is never seen, plays the bad guy who won't let the salesperson make any concessions to you. The salesperson will go back and forth to his manager's office and always come back saying he did everything he could to get what you wanted, but the manager refuses to budge.

When you encounter this duo during negotiations, the bad guy will attempt to intimidate you and is sure to reject every offer you make—he may even rush out of the room in a huff. Then, the good guy will come to the rescue and will let you know he's on your side. Because this technique is not difficult to identify, you'll be able to counter it right away. There are several ways to do this:

- **Tell them that from here on out you want to negotiate with the good guy only.** By eliminating the bad guy, the plan becomes useless.
- **Call them on it.** Ask them how long they plan on playing the good guy/bad guy performance for you. They'll get embarrassed, and the bad guy will suddenly disappear.

- **Play along.** Pretend to be alarmed by their statements, and then call off the negotiation altogether. As soon as you begin packing your briefcase, they'll be asking you to come back to work it out.

- **Develop your own bad guy.** Tell them you'd be more than happy to agree to their demands, but you have a supervisor who never bends the rules. You can get creative with how rough and tough you make your bad guy out to be.

- **Tell the good guy you'd like to speak to him privately.** Once alone, tell him you're about to walk away from this negotiation because of the bad guy's behavior and lack of professionalism. Tell him you're taking a five-minute break and expect that he will talk with his partner and advise him to back off.

Remember to employ one of these methods as soon as you know you're being duped. Getting the bad guy out of the picture early in the game allows the rest of the negotiation to progress.

The Straw-Man Technique

Straw-man techniques involve making the other party believe something is valuable to you when it really isn't. Each concession made during the negotiations is made to seem like the negotiator is giving up a lot, even if that's not actually the case. Negotiators who rely on the straw-man technique never let on that the concession they are making isn't that big of a deal.

Let's say that during the negotiation process of selling your house the buyers want you to include the washing and drying machine in the sale. Since you already planned on buying a new set for your new house, leaving the old washer and dryer at the house was something you already considered doing. But instead of telling the buyer that, you display an attitude of concern and contemplation. Let them think this is a tough decision for you to make so you can use this concession in exchange for one of theirs. You can say you'll include the washer and dryer if they take responsibility for getting the broken tiles in the bathroom fixed. You might even try **bundling** concessions to get them to both fix the tiles and replace the towel rod on the wall.

BUNDLE: Bundling is a clever way of getting the other party to make two or more concessions at once by clustering them together so they seem contingent upon each other.

Another example of the straw-man tactic is using an unnecessary delay to trade for something else of value. For example, the other party will tell you that they need more time to sleep on an issue, but then offer to give you a decision right away—in exchange for a concession. When you hear that offer, you'll know that they really don't need to take the extra time to make up their minds. What they're doing is using the straw-man technique.

One way to counter the straw-man tactic is to let the other party make all the offers first. This allows you to ask questions that reveal their needs and concerns, and leaves you in a position to use the straw-man tactic on them. Another method is to make them feel guilty for bluffing by commenting on how you're looking forward to building a positive relationship with their company and anticipate being part of the growth that your company and theirs will be sharing. Also let them know that there are great opportunities for both companies to work together again in the future. After hearing these statements, the other party will be less likely to use the straw-man tactic because he doesn't want to risk jeopardizing the trust you share and therefore also jeopardizing the possibility of more business.

"One-Time Only" Offers

Remember all that time and effort you put into preparing yourself for this negotiation? Well, don't let it all go to waste by succumbing to a phony take-it-or-leave-it tactic that turns your hard work into something that was done in vain. This is a common ploy meant to make you feel like there's an enormous amount of pressure on you to close the deal quickly.

We simply do not perform at our best in high-pressure situations; our thought process speeds up to such a rate that there isn't enough time to think things through. When a negotiator approaches you with a "one-time only" offer, he's trying to catch you off guard and is most likely **bluffing**. By telling you, for example, that you have two hours to make a decision, he's not giving you the appropriate amount of time to do additional research, consult your team, or weigh the pros and cons of the situation. You're also not given the chance to ask important questions or reassess your goals and objectives.

BLUFF: If you're a poker player, you know this word well. To bluff is to mislead via a display of strength or self-confidence. If you've done your research on your opponent, you should be able to recognize or at least suspect when they might be using this tactic on you.

When the other party introduces this tactic into the discussion, ignore it. Continue talking about the issues that were brought up or start talking about other ones. Remember, he's only trying to intimidate you. Show him you won't be manipulated in this way by refusing to acknowledge his insistent request.

In some cases, the other party's speech will speed up considerably. He might begin to talk fast and make short, blunt statements to emphasize his point even further. Don't let yourself be bulldozed; slow him down, ask questions, and most importantly, don't be forced into closing a deal if you're not ready.

On rare occasions when the other party really is in a crunch for time, try to get an extension on the deadline. Whether it's for an extra day or for an extra week, any additional time will give you the opportunity to weigh your alternatives and re-examine your goals to see if they're being met.

If your requests for more time are denied, **let the other party know what your concerns are**, and try to develop specific solutions that help eliminate the need for a deadline. At this point in the discussion, if the other party still continues to impose a strict deadline on you, show them that you won't be pressured into making overnight decisions by calling off the negotiation.

Game Delay

The opposite of the deadline ploy is the **delay** tactic. Delay tactics are used by negotiators in a variety of ways: to stall, to test your urgency, or to temporarily appease you. It's okay to give the other party some time to absorb everything so they feel comfortable about the decisions they're about to make, but **set a limit**. Don't let them take advantage of you.

DELAY: To delay something is to cause it to slow or stop. Delays are often used as a strategy to stall a negotiation or to gain more time than is probably needed. While this is a common tactic that doesn't necessarily hurt the other party, it can get out of hand.

▶ **Stalling Negotiations**

Stalling brings negotiations to a halt. By digging her heels in the ground, the other party decides she simply cannot go any further because your requests are unacceptable. Naturally, you'll begin to think about what concessions you can offer in order to keep the negotiation moving forward. However, before you start thinking about whether you can be a little more flexible, ask her point-blank what she would consider to be acceptable. Find out exactly what the obstructing element is, and try to work the issue out before you give her anything more.

▶ **Testing Urgency**

You'll want to be careful about how you react to the other party's delay because there may be only one reason he's using it: to see how desperate you are for his business. It may seem like a silly game, but sometimes you have no choice but to play along. When you do, it'll go something like this. The other party calls for a delay, you agree, then nothing happens. No phone calls. No e-mails. No contact of any kind. If you initiate contact, say the next day, the other party will know that you have no alternatives, that he has the upper hand, and that he can get more concessions out of you.

As tough as it might be, you really need to wait this one out and let him come to you. Even more difficult is determining how long you should wait for a response. While you don't want to seem eager, you don't want to let too many days slip by without hearing a word.

If you feel secure with the other options you have in place, make contact after a few days and let him know you're not happy with what he's doing. Motivate him to give you a decision by giving him a deadline; tell him all deals are off the table if you don't have his answer by a specified time.

▶ The Check Is in the Mail

We've all heard that one before! Somewhere on a continent yet to be discovered, there stands a mailbox, overstuffed with all those checks that somehow had the wrong addresses on them.

This six-word phrase was designed to give the person on the receiving end a false sense of security. A negotiator uses this tactical delay not to pressure you but to take the pressure off himself and buy more time to fulfill his obligation.

Sometimes the system is slow (checks are processed elsewhere and therefore take awhile to be drawn), and there's nothing anybody can do about it. If you've experienced this over and over again with the same company, let them know you're not a pushover by finding something to take away from them (the report you promised, the early shipment you said you'd arrange) until they deliver.

If your mailbox is still empty (and you haven't had the good fortune to find the lost continent), take action! Visit the other party or the company you've been doing business with to say that you refuse to leave until they pay up. Sometimes legal action is necessary, but usually things can be worked out so they don't get to that point.

The Element of Surprise

In yet another attempt to throw you off guard, the other party plans what seems to you like a totally unexpected twist in the negotiation.

In an instant, he brings up new information or displays a new behavior that he hopes will generate an emotional reaction from you. The reason for this is threefold.

First, he wants to break your concentration and take you away from focusing on your objectives and achieving your goals. By suddenly erupting into a fit of anger, for example, he intends to stir up your emotions and hopes that you respond with fear, shock, or frustration. If you take the bait and respond with an equal amount of anger, it may be a while before you get back to discussing the issues at hand.

Second, he anticipates your negotiation efforts to be thrown off-kilter once you let your guard down and give him an emotional response. If, for example, you react with anger, you may say something that he can use against you later when he's trying to deflate your character or prove one of his points.

Lastly, he tries to get an emotional outburst from you because he's hoping for the possibility that you'll concede something you previously did not want to concede. For example, if you react with shock or fear, you might be more likely to agree with him on an issue you were struggling with earlier.

Luckily, there are several ways to counter this assault on your emotional well-being:

- **Do not react.** Since that's exactly what the other party is hoping for, simply do not give in to his ploys. Stay calm and show your professionalism.
- **Take a break.** Give yourself time to let the new information sink in or to cool off.
- **Ask for details.** Learn as much as you can about the new information you've just been given, and determine if it's truly something to be worried about.
- **Call for help.** If the other party introduces new information to the negotiation and you're not prepared to handle it, get together with your team to discuss how to handle the new information.

Sometimes the surprise can be that a party member, usually a supervisor, is unable to attend one of the meetings so he sends another person to take his place. This person then tries to tire you out by asking you to bring him up to speed on the negotiation and to answer all his questions about why you're not being flexible on a particular issue. By prodding you for the same information over and over again, he's hoping you get so drained by the process that you'll just give into his concessions without putting up another fight.

False Concessions

A **false concession** is just what it sounds like: The other party is trying to trick you into thinking he's making a special offer just for you. For example, let's say you walk into a store to look at the gorgeous jacket you saw in the window. A salesperson approaches you and says, "The jacket costs $75, but for you, I'll sell it for $65." She wants to let you know up front that she's giving you the deal of the century on this thing. You smile politely and go back to the jacket to look over the pockets and buttons, when suddenly she says, "Ok, it seems you really like this jacket, so I'll give it to you for $55." Another discount? Now you're really interested! You inquire about the fiber content, wash instructions, and so on, and the salesperson reduces the price another $10. Feeling like you just hit the jackpot, you pay for the jacket and leave a satisfied customer. Five minutes later another prospective customer walks into the store and starts looking at the jacket. The keen salesperson says, "The jacket costs $85, but for you, I'll sell it for $75."

In both instances, the seller had a set figure in her mind the whole time. By **exaggerating** the price and then handing out a few concessions, she made it seem like you got a great bargain right there on the spot.

EXAGGERATE: To exaggerate is to represent something disproportionately to the truth. This includes both overstating and understating. If something sounds too good (or too bad) to be true, it probably is.

When you encounter a situation in which a concession is made at the onset of a negotiation, there are a few things to be aware of before you make a decision. Is the seller asking for anything in return? If not, chances are that it's not a real concession. Is the dollar amount being significantly lowered or are you given a range? If the salesperson has switched to a price range, chances are she won't come down in price beyond the range offer.

Add-Ons and Nibbling

These two tactics are a bigger deal than their names suggest. When used in negotiations, they're made to sound like small requests that don't deserve the attention larger issues usually require. If you're not careful, this misconception can cause you to give away a lot more than you think.

An **add-on** is a small concession that a negotiator asks for and adds to the end of a larger concession that's already being discussed. For example, "I'll buy your product if you throw in a free one-year warranty." If you never intended to give the free warranty, do not feel pressured to do so now. Similarly, do not feel like you were "taken" if you do decide to agree to the concession. Just make sure it's something you feel comfortable with before giving in to the other party.

Nibbling is a term used to describe the manner in which a negotiator will ask for "one last thing" after you've already reached a mutually beneficial agreement. These kinds of people are rarely ever satisfied with the agreements that have been made, and they always need to ask for another concession, and another, and another. He'll usually use excuses like, he "forgot to ask before" or "something has suddenly come up" and he needs to make a change or two.

The only way to stop these tactics in their tracks is to confront them head on. If you notice that the negotiator is continuously asking for extras, especially after everything has been finalized, simply ask him if he's happy with the deal the way it is. If he says yes, then tell him you feel that a fair settlement has been made and you see no reason to make any more changes. Usually he'll back down at this point because he feels like he gave it his best shot and can live without the concession. If he doesn't back down, ask him if you can make some changes as well.

Key Words in This Chapter
- Tactic
- Bundle
- Bluff
- Delay
- False concession
- Exaggerate
- Add-on
- Nibbling

Key Phrases in This Chapter
- Let the other party know what your concerns are.
- Set a limit.
- Do not react.
- Take a break.
- Ask for details.
- Call for help.

Case Study—Tricks, Traps, and Tactics

Let's say you're discussing doing a deal with a new vendor. You're dealing with two salespeople: Mr. Bark and Mr. Bright. The conversation might go something like this:

Mr. Smallbiz: Thanks for taking the time to discuss this with me. We're very interested in the services your company has to offer, and I hope we can come to an arrangement.

Mr. Bark: Let's get going with this. We don't have much time. We've got two more meetings this afternoon with other companies.

Mr. Smallbiz: Certainly. Now, as you know we're looking for a supplier who can provide us with 5,000 widgets a month, increasing to 8,000 widgets a month in April when our other four stores are up and running. In other words, for the year we're looking at . . .

Mr. Bark: Eighty-four thousand units for the year. Yes, I know that. I can count. Let's get on with it.

Mr. Bright: Well, let's not get too impatient, Mr. Bark. I'm sure Mr. Smallbiz has prepared very thoroughly for this meeting.

Mr. Bark: Just get on with it, okay. I've got a lot to do. Eighty-four thousand units is possible, but we'd have to put on an additional shift when you increase your demand. So the smallest number we can meet is fifteen cents per widget.

Mr. Smallbiz: What? But the number I was quoted . . .

Mr. Bark: That's the number we can do. Take it or leave it.

Mr. Bright: Mr. Bark, why don't you go take care of your other meeting and I'll keep things going here.

Mr. Bark: Okay. But remember what I said: Fifteen cents a unit. That's the bottom line. (*Leaves*)

Mr. Bright: Mr. Smallbiz, I'd like to apologize for Mr. Bark's attitude. He's under a lot of pressure just now, and I'm sure he didn't mean to sound like that.

Mr. Smallbiz: I can excuse being under pressure, but there was no call at all to behave that way. Frankly, if this is the way he's going to behave, I'm not sure I can do business with you.

Mr. Bright: Well, I'm sure you and I can work something out. Now what unit price did you have in mind?

Mr. Smallbiz: What I was thinking was . . .

Mr. Bright: I'm sorry to interrupt, but I did want to say that I think Mr. Bark's number of fifteen cents per unit is a bit high. I know he wants to hold the line on that, but between you and me I think we could come down a bit, since we're very anxious to have your business.

Mr. Smallbiz: What number were you thinking you could get to?

Mr. Bright: Well, I can't promise anything until I talk to Mr. Bark—and you saw what *he's* like—but I think we could probably go down to eleven cents a unit. It might take a bit of arguing on my part, but I think I could get him to go that low if I catch him at the right time.

Mr. Smallbiz: Well, that sounds pretty reasonable. But **let me tell you what my concerns are**. My CFO is pretty rigid when it comes to the numbers. And he's said that we'd really need these widgets to come in at eight cents a unit.

Mr. Bright: That's a very low price. I don't know if we could sustain that.

Mr. Smallbiz: I see. Well, I understand. Thanks a lot for your time.

Mr. Bright: Wait just a minute. Let me punch up some numbers here. I think with a little bit of creativity on our part, we could get to nine cents a unit. Would that work for you?

Mr. Smallbiz: I think so. The CFO might put up a bit of a fight, but I can tell him that you went to the mat for me here, so I think he'd go along.

Mr. Bright: I'd certainly appreciate that. Now, could we discuss delivery dates?

Mr. Smallbiz: Sure. It takes approximately ten days for units to be processed through our warehouse and shipped to our outlets. So we'd need to take delivery of the first shipment of widgets on December 1 so they can be in stores by December 11.

Mr. Bright: Normally that would be fine, but because that's in the middle of the holidays we're going to have to charge a shipping premium of $2,000.

Mr. Smallbiz: That's significantly higher than our other vendors. Could we get that down a bit?

Mr. Bright: We can't lower it, but I can certainly throw in something extra—for instance, we could extend the warranty on the first shipment of units an extra week.

Mr. Smallbiz: That's generous, but I understand that your company pretty much always extends the warranty for first-time shipments; that's what you've done for your other customers. So it sounds as if you wouldn't be really giving us anything special.

Mr. Bright: What did you have in mind instead?

Mr. Smallbiz: How about an extended warranty on the first three months' shipments?

Mr. Bright: Let's say the first two months. Then I think we've got something.

Mr. Bark: (re-entering) Okay, let's get back to business. Mr. Smallbiz, I've been talking to some of my people. And the units you want will have to be tied to a shipment of our widgetwinders.

Mr. Smallbiz: What do you mean?

Mr. Bark: I mean that if you want to take consignment of the widgets, you'll also have to accept a consignment of widgetwinders with them.

Mr. Smallbiz: This is the first I've heard of this.

Mr. Bark: Look, I'm tired of talking about this. If you take the widgets, you take the winders. Okay? Yes or no.

Mr. Smallbiz: (after a pause) Mr. Bark and Mr. Bright, I think the best thing here would be to take a break. Let's stop for ten minutes while I make some phone calls to my people and then we can start over again. In light of this new information, we'll have to see on what terms we can still do a deal.

Some things to notice:

1. Mr. Bark and Mr. Bright are playing a classic good-cop/bad-cop routine with Mr. Smallbiz. It's very possible that they've worked all this out before Mr. Smallbiz even walked into the room.

2. Mr. Smallbiz, cleverly, doesn't fall for it. Instead, he counters with two tactics: first, he creates his own bad cop (the omi-

nous CFO); second, he threatens to break off negotiations, which quickly brings Mr. Bright back to the table.

3. Each party makes concessions, but Mr. Bright tries to make a false concession—something he would have given away anyway—in the form of the extended warranty agreement. Mr. Smallbiz calls him on it and gets things back on track.

4. Mr. Bark tries to put Mr. Smallbiz off his stride by interrupting the negotiations and throwing in a new twist: the add-on of the widgetwinders. Mr. Smallbiz, sensibly, doesn't react. Instead he asks for some time out for everyone to cool down. Once they reconvene, he'll be in a better position to negotiate from the head rather than from the gut.

Chapter 5

The Balance of Power

BARGAINING POWER IS DEPENDENT on an endless number of components, all of which work together to create the leverage you will use during the negotiating process. The biggest misconception about bargaining power is that one side has more of it than the other side. The truth is, both sides have strengths and weaknesses that should be acknowledged by both parties and used to their advantage to create solutions that work all around the table.

When You're the Underdog

Let's say the other party has a prestigious reputation, is a long-acknowledged expert on the subject of your discussion, has superior negotiating skills, and has a stellar team backing him up. You have none of these advantages. This makes you the **underdog** in the negotiations. You can still do well, but you'll need to do a lot of research and put in a lot of time and determination into the negotiation.

UNDERDOG: An underdog is a person or team of people who are at a disadvantage and therefore expected to lose a contest or conflict

But remember, while the odds may be stacked against the underdog, that doesn't mean he can't win.

Don't let yourself be intimidated by all those credentials. Use this book to empower yourself. You'll start to believe in yourself and your abilities, and the other party will seem less threatening to you. **Your goal is to walk into the negotiation as if you couldn't possibly fail.** Give yourself the momentum of an experienced negotiator by toughening up your mental skills and working diligently at building up your confidence level.

As you go through the preparation stage of negotiating, be aware of where you can acquire leverage. Study your counterpart's competition by looking for ways they can both damage and help her. If any of your concessions can give the other party a jump on her competition, that's a plus on your side. Map out a plan on how you can use this concession as a source of strength, what you're willing to give up for it, and whether your counterpart can do without it or bargain for it with one of her other alternatives. If you are the only person who is able to give her what she wants, you have more of an advantage than you thought.

▶ How to Build More Leverage

Timing and deadlines, discussed in Chapter 2, can be used to your benefit if the other party is under strict company-imposed limitations or under contract to deliver goods and services at a specified date and time. If you have a concession that advantageously affects the other party's timeline, your offer is going to become very attractive.

Likewise, **try to predict what issues your counterpart will be most interested in**. A good place to start is at the heart of what all people in business focus on:

- Money
- Profitability

- Reputation
- Gain
- Loss

Look for concessions that fall into these categories, and use them to appeal to the other party's most imperative goals and his means of reaching them. If you sense he's taking advantage of your underdog position, remind him that you're well aware of the leverage you have by focusing his attention on how what you have to offer fits into the above points.

Sometimes the other party is overconfident and figures that since you're the underdog, you should easily give up your concessions to him. If you experience this situation, make it clear that you will not settle for an unsatisfactory agreement. No matter how unpleasant the other party might be to work with—using status as an excuse to be rude, belittling, uncompromising, or impatient—don't cave in. If you do, you'll only confirm his assumptions about your weakness and the entire negotiation will go downhill from there. Instead, stand up for yourself and let it be known that you won't be steamrolled. Your counterpart will begin to take you more seriously and will have more respect for you in the long run.

▶ Master Your Field

If lack of knowledge about the issues at hand makes you the underdog, take it upon yourself to bridge the gap. Attend a seminar or workshop that teaches negotiating skills. Take classes at your local college, and meet with specialists in the field to gain as much hands-on experience as possible. Become proactive by networking at the office and other appropriate meeting spots, and do something that gives you a little bit of recognition, like publishing an article in the newspaper.

All of these examples are immediate ways to **compensate** for some of the strengths you lack. Sure, it takes years to build a reputation, something you obviously can't do by the time you meet with your counterpart. However, get the ball rolling by making contact with your peers now. The information and advice you can get from them today could prove to be invaluable for the deals of tomorrow.

COMPENSATE: To compensate is to make up for. We all have our weaknesses, but we also have ways of balancing them out. Doing extra research, taking a class to hone your skills, and highlighting the assets you bring to the bargaining table are all ways of compensating for any weak areas in your side of the negotiation.

If You're Not Ready Yet

Simply put, **if you're not ready to negotiate, don't do it**. Maybe you need more time to prepare, or maybe you need more information from the other party. Whatever the reason, do not put yourself in a position you'll regret later. Let your counterpart know you're not ready, and if he still persists on beginning the meeting, give him an exact date you'll be ready so he knows you're not purposely putting it off.

▶ **Be Upfront**

Lying about the circumstances that are causing your delay or making up excuses to drag out proceedings will be viewed as unfair conduct. The other party might even suspect that you have entered into the negotiations in **bad faith**. If you have a situation that prevents you from going forward as planned, remember the golden rule: Do unto others as you would have them do unto you. Tell the truth, apologize for the inconvenience, and ask when might be a good time to reschedule. Do your best to estimate how long you will need—a week, a month, or more. The other party will appreciate the courtesy and will probably be more likely to be flexible.

BAD FAITH: When a party enters into a negotiation she doesn't plan to complete or makes concessions she has no intention of fulfilling, she is acting in bad faith, or deceiving the other party into thinking she is serious about the negotiation. Good faith is just the opposite, and the ideal: the implication that everyone will be fair and truthful in order to satisfy the purpose of the negotiation.

▶ **Ask for What You Need**

If you need additional information from the other party, ask them to provide this to you. Explain how these details, for example fixed percentage rates, will help you solve the conflict that's preventing you from beginning the negotiation process. Your counterpart should have no problem acquiescing to your request, and if he does, find out why. The answer you receive could be another important factor for you to consider before making your offer.

If you find yourself in a difficult situation (death in the family, illness), give yourself enough time to fully recover before you start making deals. **You need to be clear-headed, focused, and reactionary.** That's hard to do if you can't stop crying or if you're incessantly coughing and sneezing. Your disposition will also distract the other party, and it could incite her to take advantage of you.

One Winner, One Loser

A **win-lose** outcome results when positional negotiating tactics dominate the majority of the bargaining process, whereby one person thinks she got the better deal over the other. This comes about because both parties have their feet firmly planted on either side of the fence, and neither one is willing to move. They act irrationally toward each other, using pride and arrogance to focus on their ultimate goal of satisfying the **ego** instead of focusing on a positive solution for both parties.

EGO: A person's ego is his sense of self, including his self-esteem and self-image. That sounds commonplace and innocent enough, but when egos get inflated and parties stop working toward a win-win solution, a negotiation can get derailed and leave one or both parties feeling frustrated and unsatisfied.

This behavior is catastrophic for business dealings because hardly anything good ever comes out of it, even for the person who thinks she's won. In retrospect, both parties will hopefully understand that nobody walked away feeling satisfied. Because they focused on maintaining their positions, they could not establish trust or communicate their goals and objectives. **When winning becomes more important than finding the best solution, both parties will suffer.** Frustration more than anything else will serve as the catalyst for making and agreeing to concessions, in which the competition becomes a game of "the more I get, the less I have to give."

When No One Wins

Also known as a **lose-lose** outcome, deadlock occurs when negotiations come to an impasse, in which both parties have used up all their concessions. Progress seems out of reach, and disappointment fills the room because it seems like no matter how many times you go over the issues, favorable solutions are nowhere in sight. Both parties lose because neither side accomplished the main goals they set out to achieve. Additionally, emotional responses to the **stalemate** could include anger and blame, and what follows is a collapse of communication.

STALEMATE: A stalemate is any position or situation in which no action can be taken or progress made. Stalemates are common in negotiation and usually signify that a concession needs to be made or that all parties should take a break and rework their strategies.

The one good thing about deadlock is that it's not always permanent. There are ways to get around it if you stay calm and allow your mind to be open to a variety of different possibilities. **One of the main reasons for deadlock is that the best possible solution hasn't been discovered yet.** If the other party is not playing fair and refuses to be more flexible than she's been, chances are there's something she's holding onto that could possibly breathe new life into the discussion and take it out of deadlock status. She may or may not know that she has this element, so it's up to you to try to get it out of her. Get everyone in the room to start brainstorming and warm up their creative-thinking skills.

Another way to try to get out of deadlock is to take a break by getting something to eat or drink or going for a walk. When everyone comes back, see what you can resolve with the smaller issues before you get back to the deadlock problem. It'll serve as a warm-up for when the larger issue does come up again.

Knowing When to Opt Out

Sometimes, no matter how much time you've invested into making a deal work, there comes a point where you realize you want to walk away. The reasons might be readily apparent—you're not satisfied with the final offer; you turned up information about the other party that makes you uncomfortable about entering into an agreement with her; one (or more) of your alternatives presented a better offer; or you want to take an extended period of time to do more research and seek out a better alternative (if you don't have one already).

Other reasons are more psychological or intuitive. For example, if your counterpart has been quarrelsome, demanding, rude, and downright difficult to work with from the very beginning, you'll have to determine if this is the kind of person you have the patience and stamina to handle throughout the life of the contract, because it's likely his behavior will not improve in the long run. If problems arise in the future, he may prove to be just as ornery than he was throughout the negotiation period (if not more so).

The price you have to pay to settle a negotiation might not always be a harrowing experience, but it can be a financial burden. If you're not careful, you can end up doling out an exorbitant amount to attorneys and the like for fees, commissions, and anything else that might warrant a price tag. If the bill for these services is considerably more than the magnitude of your deal, consider bowing out gracefully.

Intuition, grossly undervalued by some people because of its subjective nature, plays a significant role in negotiation. People distrust intuition because they are unable to legitimize it with tangible evidence, and they aren't comfortable with relying on it. Even if you're not used to reacting on instinct alone, pay attention to any signs or "bad feelings" you experience during the meeting and investigate a little further. If the other party makes you uncomfortable for reasons you're not yet aware of, talk to the people he works with to see what you can learn. You might be surprised to discover how badly he treats his employees or how ruthless he is with his peers.

Key Words in This Chapter
- Underdog
- Compensate
- Bad faith
- Win-lose
- Lose-lose
- Ego
- Stalemate

Key Phrases in This Chapter

- Your goal is to walk into the negotiation as if you couldn't possibly fail.
- Try to predict what issues your counterpart will be most interested in.
- If you're not ready to negotiate, don't do it.
- You need to be clear-headed, focused, and reactionary.
- When winning becomes more important than finding the best solution, both parties will suffer.
- One of the main reasons for deadlock is that the best possible solution hasn't been discovered yet.

Case Study—Be Prepared

Let's consider the dangers of entering a negotiation unprepared and without a clear sense of what you want and how to get it. Meet Mrs. Eatwell, who owns a small chain of restaurants. Recently she's been approached by the owners of a much larger restaurant chain about merging the two businesses. As the curtain rises, Mrs. Eatwell, who's been too busy to properly prepare for this negotiation, is meeting with Ms. Executive, representing the Big Kahuna restaurant company.

Ms. Executive: Good morning, Mrs. Eatwell. Nice to see you. Well, let's get down to business, shall we?

Mrs. Eatwell: Uh, sure.

Ms. Executive: Now, we've already gone over in our previous meeting the advantages to both of us of a merger between our two organizations. I suggest in this meeting we drill down a bit and talk about some specifics. We can discuss personnel, vendors, and timing. I think that should pretty well fill up our time, don't you?

Mrs. Eatwell: Sure, I guess so. Do you think we should also talk about publicity and how we're going to announce this?

Ms. Executive: No, we can save that until our next session. So. Personnel. Now what is your current headcount?

Mrs. Eatwell: To tell you the truth, I'm not quite sure. We've got five stores, and I think they each have a staff of about, uh . . .

Ms. Executive: According to my research, your total headcount is 132. Does that sound right?

Mrs. Eatwell: Yes, I think so. I'd have to verify that, but that sounds like it might be the case.

Ms. Executive: Now I'm also showing that your restaurants have staffs, respectively, of twenty-two, nineteen, twenty-six, eighteen, and twenty-nine. Is that right?

Mrs. Eatwell: Yeah, probably.

Ms. Executive: That's a total of, let me see, 114 people actually working in the restaurant. So that means that you have a corporate staff of eighteen people.

Mrs. Eatwell: Uh huh.

Ms. Executive: That's a very large staff for a relatively small organization. And once the merger goes through, some of the positions will be duplicated. So I think we need to see which of your people would be let go immediately once we announce the merger.

Mrs. Eatwell: Now, wait a minute. Why would it have to be all my people who are let go? Let's consider whether some of my staff might have more experience than your people.

Ms. Executive: Well, I have to keep in mind that we have made strong commitments to our people that this merger will benefit them. I don't see how we can turn around and tell them that the benefit is they've lost their job.

Mrs. Eatwell: Well, I've made commitments to my people too. I don't want to see people lose jobs they've worked very hard at.

Ms. Executive: Look, I don't want us to get into a stalemate over this.

Mrs. Eatwell: Neither do I. What about this: We consider which positions are duplicated and make a decision in each case based on the experience and skill set of the people involved. Then, before letting the other individual go, we try to find another place they can fit in to the organization. We give them priority over any possible new hires, and if there's just no way to keep them on board, then we let them go.

Ms. Executive: Yes, I think that would work. I suggest that the decisions about this be made by a joint committee of our two organizations. My head of HR can contact your people and set this up once we're ready to go ahead with the merger.

Mrs. Eatwell: That sounds okay.

Ms. Executive: What we'd ideally like to see for the merged organization is a staff of no more than thirty. We feel this could best serve the needs of the new company and would keep us sufficiently lean so that we'd have some room for expansion in the future if business warrants it. Is that acceptable?

Mrs. Eatwell: I think so.

Ms. Executive: Now, in regards to vendors. Your main food supplier at present is Gigafood, is that right?

Mrs. Eatwell: Yes. We've worked with them for a number of years.

Ms. Executive: Our supplier has been Supercaloric, and we have an exclusive agreement with them that extends until June two years from now. So . . .

Mrs. Eatwell: Excuse me. I think we need to look at this a different way. You were going to propose that we drop Gigafood in favor of Supercaloric, is that right?

Ms. Executive: Yes.

Mrs. Eatwell: But that breaks a long relationship that my company has had with a vendor. And I think that you'd agree that ending these sorts of relationships abruptly could cause a lot of bad feeling that's not in anyone's interests. Right?

Ms. Executive: I see your point, but I think . . .

Mrs. Eatwell: Sorry, just let me continue here a moment. Rather than make this an either/or proposition, I think it would be better if we could find a way to work this out so we both get something out of the new arrangement. I don't want to drop Gigafood, though I understand your need to maintain your contract with Supercaloric. But in the terms of that contract, there must be some provision for revisiting the contract if the structure of your organization changes. Is that the case?

Ms. Executive: Yes, I believe that's the case. I'd have to review the exact terms of the contract to be sure.

Mrs. Eatwell: So let me suggest this: For the next two years, the length of your contract with Supercaloric, they will continue to supply your restaurants. However, we'll drop certain items that they supply and instead give those to Gigafood. Essentially, both vendors will be supplying the merged chain. At the end of the two years, we can review the experience and discuss whether or not to negotiate an exclusive contract with one vendor or the other. That way we both win, and the vendors win too, because they're continuing to keep their business.

Ms. Executive: I'll have to take this back to my board, but I think that's a very workable solution, Mrs. Eatwell.

Poor Mrs. Eatwell. In the first part of the discussion, Ms. Executive ran all over her. A few things to note about this conversation:

1. In the first exchange between the two parties, we see the result of poor preparation; Mrs. Eatwell doesn't have the facts and figures at her fingertips, as does Ms. Executive. The result is that she comes off stronger and gets what she wants.

2. Ms. Executive takes control of the meeting from the beginning, effectively setting the agenda and thus gaining the upper hand in the negotiation.

3. Initially Mrs. Eatwell's responses tend to be in the form of questions or tentative responses. It's not until the second half

of the conversation that she asserts herself. When she does, the negotiation swings back in her direction, and she's able to win some points.

4. Mrs. Eatwell finds a way out of the stalemate by proposing a solution in which both parties gain something.

Chapter 6

Clinching the Deal

WHEN YOU'RE IN THE thick of a negotiation, it's easy to get caught up swapping concessions and making offers and counteroffers. You're trying to keep up with deciphering the other person's body language, mood, sincerity, and next move. You must constantly take stock of how much leverage you have, re-evaluate where you stand with your give-and-takes, and reaffirm that your goals are being met. No wonder you may forget there's an end in sight! It's a long, arduous road to travel, but the final destination is worth putting up with the occasional bump or two.

Know What to Expect

You can expect a lot to happen during the final stages of a negotiation. Consequently, you'll have to rely on your business sense to pick up on important clues that surface when closure is near. If you've been studying the steps in this book, you will have indeed been applying your new skills every step of the way and should be able to recognize the tactics you've learned as they appear. Although the knowledge you've acquired thus far can be applied at this stage, there are some additional techniques and points you'll want to know.

▶ Keep It Separate from the Rest

Closing is one step in the process, and for that reason it should be treated as a separate matter. It comes with its own set of obstacles you'll need to get around and involves a great deal of creative thinking. Regard it as a review of everything you and the other party have discussed. Some agreements could have been made so long ago (hours, days, months), they'll need to be reiterated and verified.

When you're ready to close, ask your counterpart if he agrees. If so, clearly state that everything you'll be discussing from here on out will be part of the closure. Some negotiators handle closing with a completely different mindset and a totally different approach, so give them the courtesy of preparing themselves for it instead of unexpectedly springing it on them.

▶ Working Through Objections

Since closure requires the go-ahead from both parties, problems could arise if one party objects to one or more of the terms. In this case, you'll have to use your best negotiating skills to work through the objections and preclude deadlock. As frustrating as it might be, don't lose your cool by displaying aggressive or condescending behavior. You're close to the end—the last thing you want to do is jeopardize the relationship and hinder clear decision-making. Acknowledge that the disagreements are sound, even if you don't think they are, and your counterpart is more likely to treat you with the same courtesy. Work with the other party, not against her, to pinpoint where the problems lie.

If you sense there's a deeper issue than your counterpart is willing to admit, try to coax it out of her by asking questions such as, "It seems like you're feeling something isn't quite right at this point—is there another issue that concerns you?" **Be empathetic, and offer to help the other person if she needs it.**

Make sure every issue is dealt with right then and there. Otherwise, it's sure to come up again and it will be harder to resolve because you'll be even deeper into the arrangement.

When and How to Close

Though you should always be looking for opportunities to close, there are some obvious and some not-so-obvious signals that let you know when the moment is right to make this vital move. If all parties feel that their objectives have been achieved and their main goals have been satisfied, then you're ready to move on.

Similarly, if there's a solution readily available to one of the main issues you've been struggling with and both parties are in agreement, sound the horns, blow the whistles, and get the wheels rolling—you're ready to go! Another common reason for closing is a pressing deadline. Above all, if you and the other party should feel that you have settled on enough of the issues, you're ready to map out the details and close the deal.

At this point, you're probably eager to make it official—but hold on. There's one thing you need to do before concluding the negotiation period. Allow time for you and your counterpart to go over the notes you made throughout the course of the discussion. On a separate sheet of paper, outline all the agreements that were made and the details and terms that were discussed. List your concessions, the other party's concessions, concessions that were grouped together, and any **contingencies** that were made regarding these decisions. Write everything as clearly and thoroughly as you understand it to be. If everything goes smoothly, these will be the conditions of your contract.

CONTINGENCY: A contingency is an event that is dependent on the fulfillment of a condition. In a negotiation, many concessions may be contingent, or dependent, upon others. Make sure you have a full account of all of these before you make it a done deal.

Next, compare your notes with those of your counterpart, or if he didn't take notes, read each item on your list out loud. The point of this exercise is to be sure that both you and the other party understand the agreement in the same way. If you thought he was paying the shipping charges in exchange for a 20-percent discount on production fees but he thought he was paying 20 percent of the shipping, you'll want to work that out.

When things aren't going as smoothly as you hoped, and the other party is still unable to accept the conditions as they stand, offer a concession. Not a big one, but one that is worth something to them. This gesture shows the other person that you're truly giving it your best shot to make the deal work for both of you. Each of you has invested a lot of time and energy into coming up with the best deal that's in you to create; **there's no reason someone should be shortchanged**. If giving up a minor concession means something major to your counterpart and to the deal as a whole, go for it. Wouldn't you feel better walking away from the table together, to celebrate a mutual achievement instead of gloating alone about a victory? Herein lies the beauty of win-win negotiating.

Cold Feet

Cold feet isn't just an affliction that strikes brides and grooms before their weddings. As strange as it sounds, some people never want to reach the end of a negotiation. They might experience more anxiety at the closing stage than during the bargaining stage. It's a big step, not to mention a major commitment.

COLD FEET: This phrase refers to a loss or lack of courage or confidence at a crucial moment. The first recorded use of the expression occurs in Ben Johnson's play, *Volpone*, produced in 1606. By the early twentieth century, it had taken on the meaning, "to be without money," as in the case of a gambler pulling out of a poker game due to lack of cash.

Remember that feeling you had when you bought your first car? First computer? First home? After spending months researching, comparing, and reworking your budget to make the best possible purchase, you reach that part of the transaction when you're just about ready to make your dream a reality. You're excited, nervous, pensive, happy, and unsure all at once. So how are you ever going to make it through the closing with that mindset? Stop for a moment to think about how you feel and why you feel that way. Once you determine the cause of your anguish, you'll feel better about completing the deal.

▶ Overcoming Fear

Negotiating may seem intimidating at first, but once you get going, you feel more comfortable. During the negotiation process, you experience many emotions and you learn how to work through them as you resolve the issues under discussion. But when closing time nears, those old feelings seem to return to the forefront. The closing is your final step—you don't get to come back to the table tomorrow to hash out the details again. That in itself is enough to scare anyone off! But if you've been prepared the entire time, covered all your major points, and feel good about how the other party fared, then you've done your job and deserve to give yourself (and your counterpart) the opportunity to close the deal, write it down, and make it official.

If the fear won't subside, ask yourself what is making you nervous:

- Do you still feel uneasy about a particular issue?
- Are there any questions you have yet to get answered?
- Do you suspect that the other party is getting the better end of the deal?

It's natural to feel anxious, but if these questions yield no legitimate concerns or issues, take a deep breath and do what it takes to bring the negotiation to an end.

▶ **Controlling Doubt**

While questions about details like price, discounts, and deadlines are often easily answered, intangible questions that point to uncertainty and doubt can prevent you from making the commitment. You might wonder if there's more you could've done or if you should've fought harder for a particular issue. Insecurity can have you wondering if you were a pushover or if you held your own. Panic can make you feel like you've forgotten something or that you're just not ready to close.

All of these mental blocks will cause you to second-guess yourself and lose faith in a deal you felt good about closing just five minutes ago. Don't let your confidence be shattered with your own doubt. It's okay to feel apprehensive, but take control of it before it ruins what you've worked so hard to achieve.

Moreover, **by dragging your feet, you run the risk of losing your counterpart's respect and possibly the deal**. He might lose his patience or begin to have questions of his own, and the last thing you want to do is give him time to second-guess himself too. Have faith in yourself, your work, and the negotiation, and close the deal knowing you did the best you could possibly do. The key to successful negotiating isn't about how many times you can win the game. It's about careful planning, honest problem solving, and sharp instincts—all of which help you achieve the goals you set out to accomplish.

Extras and Perks

If you're ready to close but the other party is still **ambivalent**, there are a few things you can do to help ease them into closure. In addition to helping you bring your negotiation to a successful conclusion, extras and perks can help you show that you have character and an excellent business sense.

AMBIVALENCE: Ambivalence is a feeling of uncertainty resulting from the inability to make a choice or the simultaneous desire to do two opposing things. If either you or your opponent is feeling ambivalent at any point during a negotiation, one needs to do something to encourage the other to move forward.

As stated previously, you should always be trying to develop a good relationship with your counterpart, whether you're verifying information with them during the preparation stage, bargaining with them during the negotiating stage, or composing the contract together. The relationships you begin building today will over time blossom into great friendships and successful partnerships that both of you continuously benefit from. There may be other opportunities for you to work together. By establishing good business practices now, you're ensuring favorable results for the future.

A little enthusiasm goes a long way, especially when your counterpart shows hesitation. Just a few encouraging words may be just what she needs to hear to move on. You can also point out all the objectives the other party has accomplished. Sometimes hearing them listed out loud makes a bigger impact than just quietly thinking them over. Go over any deadlines that were agreed on. Say something like, "By June 1st, you'll have the first shipment so you'll be able to ship to your customers way ahead of schedule." This will help the other party get a clear picture of how she benefits from the transactions that took place. Positive energy is contagious, so use it often.

As part of your planning, compile a list of several small concessions that you wouldn't mind giving up, if needed. Use them as backup for when you need to apply a little push. Your counterpart will certainly appreciate the favor, and hopefully that will be all she needs to overcome last-minute indecision.

That said, while it's good to have something in reserve for emergencies, be careful you don't give too much away. Once you've agreed to close, leave it at that. **Don't try to rehash issues you've already agreed on**—you could be opening up a can of worms. At this point in the game, you want to reassure, review, and revise if necessary, but you definitely don't want to renegotiate.

Success!

The key to great negotiating is integrity—being able to make a commitment and following through on your promises. Therefore, the key to a successful close is thinking about it from day one. Everything you do—research, planning, bargaining, relationship building—should be done with closing in mind. When doing research, think about what you can use as last-minute concessions; when planning, have backups set in place at every stage of the game, and come up with answers to "what if" questions; while bargaining, continue to move forward and take steps to avoid an impasse; and whenever possible, create a positive atmosphere and establish trust and respect by showing goodwill. You want to satisfy your goals. However, the overall goal is to get to the close and make everything official.

Closing is a separate step that requires as much **diligence** as all the other steps did. You should never rush through it. Here are the closing checkpoints you need to be sure you follow through with:

- First, confirm that everyone is in agreement, making sure everything has been worked out and there's nothing left to close. Use the list of concessions you made to once again verify all terms and conditions, if needed.
- Next, review the agenda to be sure everything has been covered and all major points have been discussed.
- Finally, create a few to-do lists, recording deadlines to follow up on and deadlines to meet.

DILIGENCE: Diligence is constant and earnest effort put toward the accomplishment of a goal. Like many things in life, negotiation requires a healthy dose of diligence to get the job done right. Put in solid effort every step of the way, and you'll be doing your best to ensure the desired outcome.

If you are able to check off those three boxes, then congratulations! The closing is finished, and it's time to sign the contracts. Grab your finest champagne glasses along with your favorite ballpoint pen and make a toast to yourself, your counterpart, and the success of your negotiation. Reward yourself for all your hard work—go out for dinner, throw yourself a party, celebrate! You've certainly earned it.

Key Words in This Chapter
- Contingency
- Cold feet
- Ambivalence
- Diligence

Key Phrases in This Chapter
- Be empathetic, and offer to help the other person if she needs it.
- There's no reason someone should be shortchanged.
- By dragging your feet, you run the risk of losing your counterpart's respect and possibly the deal.
- A little enthusiasm goes a long way.
- Don't try to rehash issues you've already agreed on.
- The key to great negotiating is integrity.

Case Study—Closing with Confidence

Even at the end of a deal, things can go wrong. But, as we'll see here, there are ways to make sure your closing stays on track and you finish with an agreement that works for both of you. Let's listen in on two executives negotiating a new partnership agreement between their firms.

Ms. Bigshot: Okay, I think we've got these numbers wrapped up. We're in agreement on the basic points here, right?

Mr. Indecisive: Well, I think so, but I'm still a bit concerned about how the weekly exchange of sales numbers is going to work. Because we don't update our numbers until Friday, but you said you needed the information on Thursday.

Ms. Bigshot: Right. We went over that, if you remember. We can push our reporting deadline back a day to accommodate your schedule.

Mr. Indecisive: Oh, yes, that's right.

Ms. Bigshot: So I think we can move to close this up at this point. Let me just reiterate the main points of agreement: We'll begin this partnership on March 6, and it will run for eighteen months. At the end of that time, we'll reevaluate and determine whether we want to continue or not. During the eighteen months, your customers will receive our widgets at a 20-percent discount, and our customers will be able to purchase widgetwinders at a 15-percent discount, with an extra 5-percent discount on orders of 500 or more. We'll announce this agreement in a press release this Saturday. . . .

Mr. Indecisive: Wait, wait. Did we agree to that timing?

Ms. Bigshot: Yes. We talked about this before, that we want to get the word out quickly so our customers can begin to make their purchase plans before the summer selling season hits.

Mr. Indecisive: Yes, I remember we talked about that. But I'm still nervous about it. I mean, I've got to get this past our board, and I wonder if they're going to be very quick to approve it.

Ms. Bigshot: I see your point. Is there anything I can do to help? For instance, I could pull together some of the figures I presented to you at our last meeting and put them in a PowerPoint presentation that you could show to the board. I'd also be happy to draw up a memorandum from our board summarizing the advantages of this arrangement in terms of increased revenue for both companies.

Mr. Indecisive: Yes, that would be helpful. I'd appreciate it.

Ms. Bigshot: Great! Consider it done.

Mr. Indecisive: But do you think we should wait another couple of weeks before finalizing everything? Just to give this deal time to settle and let everyone think about it some more.

Ms. Bigshot: We could do that, but I think we'd be throwing away an opportunity. The truth of the matter is that deals like this depend heavily on timing, and if we don't move now it raises questions about whether it's worth setting up this partnership at all.

Mr. Indecisive: Yes, I see your point. And I assure you, we really do want to do this.

Ms. Bigshot: Here's my suggestion. I'll draw up a deal memorandum that embodies all the points we've agreed on. I'll send it to you by end of business day tomorrow. I'll also include the material I mentioned earlier, the facts and figures in a PowerPoint that you can submit to your board. While you're looking that over, I'll have my people start drawing up the contract. They can send over the draft to you by the day after tomorrow, and you'll have that to look at while your board is considering the issue.

Mr. Indecisive: Yes . . . yes, I think that would probably work.

Ms. Bigshot: The other thing I think we can get to work on right away is the press release. I'll have my PR people draft it and then send it on to you. That way, everything will be in place and ready to roll out Saturday when your board approves this partnership.

Mr. Indecisive: *If* they approve it, you mean.

Ms. Bigshot: No, I mean *when*. I have a lot of confidence they'll go for what we've agreed on here. I think we've done a very good, thorough job of hashing out the various issues and reviewing the numbers. I have to tell you, Mr. Indecisive, that I believe in this partnership. It's going to result in substantial sales for both our companies, and it will expand our geographic reach so that we both benefit from tapping a new customer pool.

Mr. Indecisive: You may very well be right. I know that sometimes it's hard to see the forest for the trees, and I can certainly see the benefits of this arrangement. I just don't want to get rushed into anything I'll regret later.

Ms. Bigshot: Mr. Indecisive, here's the bottom line: I've been in this business a long time, and I know you have too. We both know that trying to make bad deals doesn't benefit anyone in the end. If I didn't believe—really believe—that this deal was the right thing for both of us, I wouldn't do it. Because if it's a bad deal for you and we go through with it, I'll be destroying my relationship with your company, and that's not going to do me any good in the long run. At the end of the day, all I've got is my integrity, and I'm standing on that when I tell you that we should create this partnership. Not just because it's good for my company, but because it's good for *both* companies.

Mr. Indecisive: I believe you, Ms. Bigshot. I think we have a deal. Let's put it to bed.

At the end of a prolonged negotiation, there's nothing more annoying than someone who wants to start all over again. Fortunately, in this case, Ms. Bigshot is able to cut off Mr. Indecisive at the pass and corral him back into inking the deal. Some things to note:

1. Ms. Bigshot never loses her temper, although it must be tempting. Instead, she approaches the problem of Mr. Indecisive's wavering as a matter of finding out how to *help* the other party come to an agreement.

2. By being decisive and having plenty of suggestions, Ms. Bigshot is able to keep the tone of the discussion positive and moving forward. If she'd reacted with anger or negativity to Mr. Indecisive, it's quite possible the deal could have blown up in these closing moments. Instead, it goes ahead.

3. Ms. Bigshot suggests that her company draw up the initial drafts of all the paperwork, in this way controlling the terms of the deal.

4. A jolt of enthusiasm and a reminder of the importance of honesty in business dealings finish the meeting on a high note.

Chapter 7

Putting It in Writing

ALTHOUGH THE DETAILS OF a contract are not fleshed out until the end of a meeting, it's important to keep them in mind throughout the entire negotiation period. Taking good notes and writing down everything that's agreed upon will not only ensure you include everything you want in the contract, but it will also help clear up the hazy points that were discussed hours or even days beforehand.

All about Contracts

Contracts serve to record agreements that two or more parties have made with each other and to outline the **stipulations** of those agreements. A good contract should protect the promises, expectations, and investments of the parties involved. In fact, contracts are legal documents and hold up in court. There are literally thousands of different types of contracts, ranging from a template contract you find online to a specific contract written up following negotiations.

STIPULATION: A stipulation is a condition, demand, or promise in an agreement or contract. Before you sign anything, make sure the contract includes all of the stipulations you discussed during the negotiation period.

▶ **Form Contracts**

Form or **boilerplate** contracts are templates that represent the bare bones of a company's demands. Most real estate agencies and mortgage brokers will use the same form contract for every client, listing the conditions, limitations, and delivery expectations the company demands, amending the boilerplate only to reflect the terms and provisions unique to each situation. The set-in-stone appearance of this type of contract may seem intimidating, so it's important to keep in mind that form contracts really aren't indisputable—any part can be changed.

BOILERPLATE: A boilerplate is a basic contract that can be modified to cover various kinds of transactions. Read these contracts carefully and thoroughly, and don't skip any sections. Mark any changes you have right on the contract, and initial the changes.

Also keep in mind that boilerplates are often riddled with convoluted statements and words, such as "heretofore," "hereinafter," "thereof," "thereto," "hereof," and "in furtherance of." When you come across this type of legalese in your contract, ask for an explanation. Don't be embarrassed—*no one* (except lawyers) knows what this stuff means. Also, get the translations for any Latin phrase, like "arguendo," "ab initio," "ad rem," and "haec verba."

▶ **Drafting a Contract**

You may draft your own contract or have someone draft one for you. In the latter case, you want to follow a few simple steps. First, decide who will be the one to draw up the contract, and make sure everyone agrees whom that person will be. Next, start with a basic contract and work from there. You can either download one from the Internet or acquire one from an attorney or other legal official. Appendix C includes a list of websites that offer printable contracts. Generic forms are free, such as living wills and demand for payment letters, but the more complex forms like negotiating forms come with hefty price tags. Some websites also allow you to view sample contracts like those used for business mergers.

▶ **Note Taking**

However you and the other party choose to have the contract drawn, you should always be thinking about what information you want to be clearly stated on the form. Taking notes from the beginning of the discussion right up until the signing of the contract prevents crucial details such as the following from being left out, muddled, misconstrued, or denied:

- Your and the other party's gains—big and small
- Conditions on which these gains are based
- Referenced material, such as price lists, warranty information, or insurance policies
- Any emotional clues you picked up from the other party (especially helpful in assessing the party's sincerity and comfort level to estimate whether they'll be able to make good on a particular obligation)
- Important deadlines—both yours and the other party's
- Anything and everything pertinent to the courses of action agreed upon

Don't forget to jot down notes after each phone call, e-mail, and other communication. Also mark the date and time the initial contact took place so any changes that were discussed are on record. If not written down immediately, these things are easy to forget, especially if you're involved in a month-long negotiation process.

Deciding on Details

Putting together a contract is almost as fun as writing a user manual. The details are so minute that it's easy to zone out and overlook a few. There are some checkpoints you can put into place that will help you identify gaps as well as help you know what important information should be included.

▶ Terms of Agreement

A contract is only legal and valid if something of value is exchanged for something else of value, and both parties must agree on all the terms. Even further, some states require that these **considerations** be in writing in order for the contract to be considered a legal document.

CONSIDERATION: Consideration is basically a fancy term for benefits, gains, or promises. These are the "meat" of any contract or agreement. In signing the contract, both parties agree to all considerations listed therein.

Everything that was agreed upon, including the conditions that were placed on those agreements, should be written into the contract. This includes but is not limited to deadlines, obligations, and consequences of termination. All specific details should be clearly written out. **Say what you mean, and mean what you say.** If you enter into a contract to have your dining room painted and you expect the painter to remove the wallpaper first, make that point clear in the contract. If you want the painter to blend three particular shades of green to use as the primary color on the walls, include that statement as well. Details, details, and more details are what should be included in this section of the contract. Knowing what to expect and knowing what's expected of you reduces the likelihood of disputes later on.

▶ Unpredictable Circumstances

Make sure you and the other party know full well what the outcome will be if something unexpected happens. If there's a fire and the dining room is damaged before the painter has completed it, who will be responsible for payment? Will the contract become null and void?

Always make sure there are alternative solutions set in place. Try to imagine every possible scenario (relative to the agreement) and devise solutions that will be immediately put into action if one of the scenarios takes place. Expect the unexpected, and you'll never be left in the dark about how to handle the "what ifs."

▶ **Breaching the Contract**

Have a clause worked into the contract that states what the consequences will be if either party fails to uphold the contract, also called **breaching**. Be advised that some people enter into negotiations with every intention of breaching the contract. If a party has breached the contract, sending a notice of protest to the damaging party preserves your rights and serves as proof in a court of law that a breach has manifested.

BREACH: To breach is to break. If one party has breached the contract, they have broken it; in other words, they have violated the terms that were agreed upon. Perhaps they didn't provide the proper goods or services promised, or they didn't do it within the agreed-upon timeframe.

Another term for breach of contract is "failure of consideration." It means you didn't hold up your part of the bargain. At this point, the contract becomes null and void, and the person who has been wronged can withhold making good on her considerations and/or take legal action against the other party.

Make a List and Check It Twice

When the time comes for you to look over the contract, you'll need to pay attention. Read every word of every page, and check all the factual information (particularly the spelling of your name and the dates) for accuracy. Double-check to make sure that all agreed-upon gains for both sides are listed. If there's anything that you don't understand or that doesn't make sense, ask for a clarification. Use common sense—if the contract is too complicated, get professional help in reviewing it. If something needs to be changed, have both parties initial all changes. Sign every page, and insist on an original copy if one isn't provided to you.

▶ Understand What You Read

Surely the most frustrating part of reading a contract is translating all the mumbo jumbo. But you shouldn't be intimidated by legalese or let it prevent you from asking questions about anything you don't understand. Neglecting to ask for clarification of certain terms and statements could end up hurting you in the future. **If something doesn't make sense, ask for an explanation.** If it still doesn't make sense, ask again or ask someone else.

▶ Dos and Don'ts

Following a few dos and don'ts will help you evaluate your contract and know what should be double-checked. Use this list as a starting point to make sure you've covered your bases:

- Do crosscheck all documents and paperwork referred to in the contract.
- Do check for **amendments** the other party made—you'll need to initial these.
- Do make sure the other party has agreed to and signed your amendments.
- Do read the fine print.
- Do read all boilerplate material.
- Don't skip over sections because they look too exhausting to read.
- Don't forget to check the numbers—dates, prices, discounts, fees, and compensation.
- Don't assume that everything is correct.

AMENDMENT: An amendment is a change or addition to a document. Amendments are perfectly fair play during the contract-writing stage, but all parties must approve and initial any changes.

Rework the contract as many times as you need to until you're completely satisfied. Keep in mind that while it's okay to rework the contract, you shouldn't overwork it—you don't want to renegotiate everything if it's not necessary.

Contract Law

A lot can happen between the time you sign the contract and the time it ends. Problems could arise that put either you or the other party in danger of being unable to fulfill your obligations, and you'll need to know the best way to handle those situations. For instance, if you contracted a painter to paint your dining room in a specified amount of time and he didn't show up on the last day to complete the job, how long should you wait before contacting a lawyer? Are you entitled to compensation if you entered into an agreement with a person whose nonperformance cost you money?

Contract law answers these and other questions about your rights as party to a contract. It represents all parties who are responsible for meeting the terms as specified in the contract they signed.

▶ **Withdrawing from the Contract**

Most of us have experienced buyer's remorse at one point. You find something you like, buy it, then change your mind and decide you no longer want it. Usually, you can return the item to the store and get a refund, but it works differently with items that can't easily be returned, such as a house or a car.

When you enter into a business contract, a lot depends on what the other party is willing do to. If you want to get out of the contract, the other party might simply allow it in order to maintain the integrity of the relationship. Maybe there was an oversight on your part, such as an accounting error that won't allow you to live up to your promises, or maybe something unexpected happened and your counterpart feels cutting you loose is the better choice. She also might have the foresight to know that if she doesn't let you out of the contract now, it may be difficult for you to live up to your side of the contract, thus making it more difficult for her to operate her business.

Though your counterpart may be empathetic with your reasons for wanting to cancel the contract, she's not obliged to let you do it. If she decides not to let you out of the contract, you'll have to hire a lawyer to discuss your options.

If your counterpart wants to cancel the contract, use your judgment to decide if it's in your best interest to excuse her. In this case, you'll need a **release**.

RELEASE: A release is a document relinquishing claims, actions, and/or any rights against another party, or freeing them of any responsibilities that were stated in the original contract. For example, if you borrow someone's car for two days and sign a release that states you're not responsible for any engine damage that appears during that time period, the owner cannot sue you or expect you to pay for the repairs.

▶ Breach of Contract

A breach transpires when one party fails to perform what the contract states he has agreed to do. It occurs when the other party cannot perform her own duties, when the offending party does something that goes against what the contract states, or when the offending party simply will not do what's expected of her. You'll have to decide how severe the breach is before you decide to handle the matter in court.

For example, if your counterpart delivered goods three days past the agreed-upon ship date but the late shipment didn't harm your business, you might let it slide this time, discuss it with her to prevent it from happening again, and be on the lookout for any breaches that occur in the future. If, however, you decide that the breach is too significant to ignore, there are many options available to you—and most of them, not surprisingly, involve money.

In addition to assessing the value of your losses, the judge might require the other party to pay any attorney fees that accrued from the time the contract was breached. He might also order the other party to pay "consequential and incidental damages," money awarded for losses that were predicted if a breach occurred.

Other remedies pertain to the state of the contract itself. If the judge decides on a **rescission** of the contract, the contract is canceled, all advancements are to be paid back, and all parties are no longer responsible for their portion of the terms.

The Litigation Option

In its simplest form, **litigation** is the process of taking part in legal proceedings to solve a dispute; filing a lawsuit is engaging in litigation. There are many reasons why litigations come about—to decide who gets what in a divorce; to settle a malpractice suit; to determine who is in the wrong in an auto accident; to get someone to carry out their duties as stated in a mutual agreement, and so on. Anyone can file the claim—a small business, a large corporation, neighbors, coworkers, or governments—as long as they have an issue that they believe needs to be settled by the court system.

Not all lawsuits require an exorbitant amount of money, nor do they all take years to settle. However, they can get quite messy and complicated, especially when the parties involved cannot communicate in a civil manner, as happens all too often in a divorce. When this is the case, it gets harder to find a solution and it takes longer to work out the details of the settlement.

Filing a lawsuit shouldn't be a decision that's made in haste. Retain a lawyer to determine the best possible way to resolve your issue. While she may or may not suggest litigation, her advice is invaluable. If your decision is to sue, your lawyer will be able to tell you how much time you have to file the claim, depending on the laws in your state. She will also take you through the many steps that are required, including the prelitigation settlement discussion—a discussion which gives you and the other party another chance to reach an agreement before going to court. If a resolution cannot be made, the suit is filed and the other party responds by acknowledging that he is being sued.

Next, both parties and their lawyers will sit with the judge to discuss the basic elements of the lawsuit in a final effort to solve the issue outside of court. If this attempt fails, then a trial will be the next step, where a judgment is awarded.

Even if you've already filed a lawsuit, you can still settle the dispute on your own; once you settle, the suit will be dismissed. However, always consult a lawyer before making such a critical decision—once the suit is dismissed, it cannot be re-filed. Don't let inexperience guide you in the wrong direction.

Dispute Resolution Alternatives

Another function of contract law is to provide methods for resolving disputes outside of court. A lawsuit can be lengthy, distressing, and expensive, and the longer it drags on, the longer you'll have to wait to get results. Alternative dispute resolutions help you reach a solution faster than a lawsuit would, and there are three methods available:

- Negotiation and settlement
- Mediation
- Arbitration

The first one involves a process in which the parties discuss their dispute and hopefully reach a settlement. The last two methods involve a third party and are discussed in the following two sections.

▶ **Mediation**
Mediation is the act of settling or reconciling a matter between two parties by a third party, a mediator. While the mediator can be someone who is highly knowledgeable in the issues being negotiated or mediated, expertise isn't really necessary. Your mediator should be an expert in dispute resolution because her job is to help the disput-

ing parties find some way to reach an agreement, especially when the negotiation is in deadlock.

The mediator offers a fresh perspective on the situation, which allows her to find the solution. Because she's working for both parties, she doesn't have a strong desire to hold onto certain concessions or make demands. Instead, the position she holds is to find the best possible outcome based on the facts and objectives of the concerned parties.

Mediation is not a legal proceeding, such as a trial, and the mediator cannot decide on what the parties have to agree to. It's a casual meeting in which the mediator talks to both parties together and then separately to help them refocus their attentions on their goals and what they're willing to do to reach them. Sometimes it's easy to lose sight of the purpose of the negotiation, and that's where a mediator can help.

Mediators are brought into negotiations and disputes to avoid litigation. Although if a lawsuit has already been filed, they might be brought in to avoid accruing more lawyer and court costs. Since all parties involved share the mediator's fees, it's often the most favorable choice when considered from a financial standpoint.

Just like the contract that results from a negotiation, the agreement is documented, signed, and enforceable by law. If the agreement is reached after a lawsuit has been filed, the court will receive a copy, and the case will be dismissed.

▶ Arbitration

Arbitration is similar to mediation in that it is a type of alternative dispute resolution that involves the inclusion of an outside party to help settle the dispute. What makes this process different is that the arbitrator directs a hearing and then decides who gets what. It's almost like litigation but is faster, cheaper, and more flexible. You don't have to worry about the court dates being pushed back because other cases take precedence over yours, and the parties can decide on the rules that will be in effect throughout the arbitration period.

For example, evidence that otherwise might not be allowed in court can be submitted in arbitration. Moreover, the parties can decide on who the arbitrators will be and whether the arbitration will be binding (parties must follow the arbitrator's final decisions) or nonbinding (parties take the award under advice and do not have to carry out the final decisions). Once the arbitration is finished, the resulting decision cannot be appealed. The conflict is considered resolved, and the case is closed.

Anyone can be an arbitrator, as long as both parties agree. Typically, arbitrators are experts on the subject that is being discussed, trusted community members (such as spiritual leaders), or those who have many years of experience in law (such as retired judges or lawyers). When choosing an arbitrator, look for someone who is adept in managing arbitration hearings. Your candidate should have good written, oral, and organization skills as well as the ability to summarize information quickly and make intelligent decisions.

Key Words in This Chapter

- Stipulation
- Boilerplate
- Consideration
- Breach
- Amendment
- Release
- Rescission
- Litigation
- Mediation
- Arbitration

Key Phrases in This Chapter

- You may draft your own contract or have someone draft one for you.
- Say what you mean, and mean what you say.

- If something doesn't make sense, ask for an explanation.
- Filing a lawsuit shouldn't be a decision that's made in haste.

Case Study—The Devil's in the Details

As mentioned in the previous chapter, there are a lot of advantages to being the one to draft the contract. Even though the contract is still subject to negotiation, you've had the first chance to frame the terms of the discussion.

Let's listen in on an initial discussion of a contract between an editor and an author, trying to work out terms for publishing a book.

Mr. Editor: I sent you a copy of our contract last week, and I'm hoping you've had a chance to look at it and see that it reflected our discussions about your project.

Ms. Bestseller: Yes, I did, thanks. I've got some questions, if you don't mind.

Mr. Editor: Fire away.

Ms. Bestseller: First of all, could I ask where the language for this came from? It seems awfully, well . . . legal.

Mr. Editor: That's because it is. This is based on our standard boilerplate contract that we use with all authors. We just adapt the language and terms to the person we're negotiating with, but the basic language has been prepared by our legal team. I know it seems kind of roundabout and legalese-y, but the lawyers are concerned to protect everyone's interests. Including yours, by the way.

Ms. Bestseller: Well, I appreciate that, but just to be on the safe side I ran this by my lawyer as well, and that's where some of these questions are coming from.

Mr. Editor: Okay.

Ms. Bestseller: For instance, let's look up here in the first paragraph where it says that the Author (me) agrees to deliver a manuscript of no less than 55,000 words.

Mr. Editor: Right.

Ms. Bestseller: Didn't we agree that the manuscript would only be 45,000 words? It seems concerning to me to suddenly add 10,000 words onto a contract. After all, that's quite a lot of writing, given that the deadline is very tight.

Mr. Editor: Let me check my notes. Hmmm. It looks as if you're right. We agreed to 45,000 words. However, I'd like to keep this a little flexible. Could we say a range of 45,000 to 50,000 words?

Ms. Bestseller: I think so, but that raises another point. Here in the fourth paragraph . . .

Mr. Editor: I'm sorry to interrupt, but while we're thinking about it could you cross out 45,000 words and substitute "between 45,000 and 50,000 words" and then put your initials next to that? That'll make everything legal in the final signed document.

Ms. Bestseller: Sure. No problem. I'll make that change on all the copies of the contract before I send them back to you. But now down here in paragraph four it says that if I don't deliver by the deadline of May 1, I'll be penalized by having to forego 25 percent of the advance on the book. Considering I just agreed to possibly deliver an additional 5,000 words of text, it seems to me that it's not quite right to hold me to this deadline at the possible cost of part of the advance.

Mr. Editor: I see your point, but at the same time I have to ensure that you'll deliver the manuscript in a time frame that works for our production schedule on this book.

Ms. Bestseller: Could we push that deadline back a week to May 8? I'd be confident in delivering a completed manuscript by then, and if I don't, I'm willing to be penalized.

Mr. Editor: Yes, that would be okay. Please make that change and initial the contracts.

Ms. Bestseller: Okay. Now in this section on page five it says that royalties are based on net proceeds from sales. I don't quite understand what that means. I wonder if you could explain it to me a bit.

Mr. Editor: Sure. Bookstores buy from us on consignment, and if, after a couple of months, they need to lower their inventory for a particular book, they return the excess books to us. That's what the term "returns" refers to. Our royalty payments to you are based, as much as we can figure, on the total net sales to the bookstores—that is, our initial sell-in minus returns. Does that make sense?

Ms. Bestseller: Yes, I see now. Okay, I just wanted some clarification on that point. After all, I don't want to put my name on something I don't understand.

Mr. Editor: Absolutely. If there's anything unclear in the contract, we should get it out of the way right now.

Ms. Bestseller: So along the same lines, could you just explain what happens if I deliver the manuscript to you and you don't like it?

Mr. Editor: Well, just to be clear: If you don't deliver the book to us at all, that would be a breach of contract and we'd have the right to withhold your advance, since you broke the terms of the agreement. If you send us the manuscript and we review it and decide it's not publishable, then we'll give you some time to fix it, as specified in the contract under paragraph three. You can see that it's all spelled out there. If, after you've had time to fix it, it's still not ready to be published, then we consider you in breach of contract, since you were supposed to provide something we could publish and you didn't. If you fix it, of course, all is well and good, and we just proceed as if nothing happened.

Ms. Bestseller: I see. That makes sense. As long as I have a reasonable amount of time to fix it, of course. I see here that I have thirty days. Isn't that awfully short?

Mr. Editor: That's pretty standard in the industry. It's what we always use, because if we put things off and give you a lot more time, that can create a lot of scheduling problems for us, and ultimately that won't be good for the book's sales.

Ms. Bestseller: Well, I guess I'll just have to turn in a perfect first draft then. I think that's all the questions I had. I'll sign these and send them along to you tomorrow.

As you can see from this discussion, even at the contract stage, negotiations are continuing. You can also see that:

1. Ms. Bestseller did the right thing in asking questions about anything in the contract that was unclear. Legal language can often be convoluted, and if you don't ask what something means, you might be disappointed to find out the answer when it's too late.

2. Both Mr. Editor and Ms. Bestseller exhibited flexibility in their responses. The contract stage is no time to start practicing positional negotiating.

3. The contract clearly spells out the consequences of a breach of contract. This is essential, since both parties have to know from the start what it will mean if one or the other doesn't live up to their end of the bargain.

Chapter 8

Building Confidence and Skills

THEY SAY PRACTICE MAKES perfect, and this is certainly the case with negotiating. While you may never reach a state of perfection (we're mere mortals, after all), you can certainly work to boost your self-confidence and hone your interpersonal skills. Think of the whole world as your negotiating playground. In every store, restaurant, and office you enter—both in your own neighborhood and in your travels—there is a deal just waiting to be made. Everything truly is negotiable, and if it isn't, it doesn't hurt to ask.

Act It Out

One way to improve your negotiating skills is to create a script. Write down what you plan to say and then create a **hypothetical** situation in which you get to act out your side of the discussion. Practicing like this will give you a better idea of how you will react in certain situations. You might even discover the hidden movie star in you! To get the full effect, solicit help from another person, choosing someone who makes you feel relaxed and secure. If you're too busy worrying about what the other person thinks of you, you'll have a hard time focusing on the important details of the negotiation.

HYPOTHETICAL: A hypothetical situation is a theoretical one. Though it isn't real, it's a possibility you might consider as a way to sort out your thoughts before taking actual action. In the case of negotiating, it's always best to practice what you might say and make educated guesses about how the other party might respond to you in a given situation.

▶ Make a Speech

A great way to deliver your opening proposal is in speech form. There are many books and websites out there that can help you learn the basics, or you can talk to a friend or colleague with speech-giving experience. He or she might offer tips for getting (and keeping) the audience's attention, or suggest specific words to use to spice up your presentation.

Once you've written your speech, deliver it separately to a few different people so you get a variety of responses. Choose people with diverse personalities so you can take notes on how different personality types react. Next, ask each person what he or she liked and disliked about the speech. What words, issues, or actions did your audience find memorable? Finally, choose the responses from the person who resembles your negotiating counterpart the most. Tailor your speech to match the person's attention span and level of excitement about particular issues. If your target audience had a hard time staying focused on what you were saying, make your speech more interesting by using voice inflection, emphasis on words, and visual aids like slides or handouts.

Making an audio or, better yet, video recording of yourself as you give the speech is another great way to practice. Identify "filler" words that are used to replace uncomfortable silences. Watch out for "like," "you know," and "so," as well as murmurings like "um" and "ah." If you have a video of yourself, keep an eye out for distracting gesticulations or nervous ticks, like toe-tapping. You'll want to correct these habits if you want the other party to feel that you're confident, intelligent, and prepared.

▶ **Role-Playing**

You can have a lot of fun with this one. Not only does it provide great entertainment for family and friends, it also teaches you how to lighten up the mood when things get too serious. Tension breeds more tension, and a few playful words or a tasteful joke can break the cycle. Of course, you'll need to think about whether your counterpart is receptive to comic relief.

Another benefit of role-playing is that it helps you remember things better. When you act out various scenes, you can get really creative when playing up the drama of the situation. Start off by having another person play the role of your counterpart. Let your helper choose a negotiating role to play (such as intimidator or arguer) without telling you what it is. See if you can figure out what negotiating style the person is using and adjust your style as needed.

You can also try switching roles to get a feel for how your counterpart will be defending each of his own points and to try to predict what kinds of concessions he'll be asking for. Take all the information you've gathered about your counterpart, his company, and his goals and use it to employ the tactics you're most worried about having to counter. It will be interesting to see how your helper reacts to them, especially if he or she devises new ways of handling each ploy.

Play Devil's Advocate

Using the **devil's advocate** training technique helps you hone your skills by testing your own arguments and strategies. When preparing for a negotiation, ask someone unrelated to the situation to play devil's advocate to test your skills. The person you choose should systematically reject everything you throw his way just for the sake of doing it. His job is to point out everything that could go wrong with either the negotiation or with the issues you bring up. If you use him to critique your negotiating strategy, he'll be asking you a lot of "what if" questions: What if the other party says this? What if your tactic backfires? What if you make a mistake? When he plays the role of the other party and uses the devil's advocate method, he'll ask a lot of these same questions, as well as take the opposing side of every issue you raise.

DEVIL'S ADVOCATE: To play devil's advocate is to take a position you would not normally take with the goal of opening up a discussion to other possibilities. When preparing for a negotiation, it can be helpful to have someone play devil's advocate so that you can consider the various ways that your opponent might react to situations.

The purpose of this exercise is to prepare yourself for any doubts, concerns, and misgivings your counterpart may bring up. Having the answers ahead of time makes it easier to reassure the other party that you have thought everything through. It also makes it harder for you to be caught off guard.

Go Shopping

Love it or hate it, shopping is one of those things we all have to do. You need groceries, new clothes, school supplies for the kids, and so on. And sometimes shopping can be fun! You hit the mall with some friends on the weekend, or you try your luck at bargaining at a **flea market**. Every time you use a coupon, ask for a discount, or try to get someone to give you two items for the price of one, you're negotiating. You can't negotiate everywhere, but in some arenas, it's just how it's done. These are great opportunities not just to hone your skills but also to save some money!

FLEA MARKET: There are a few different theories about how and where this term originated, one being a large, outdoor market in Paris that was rumored to have had a critter problem in the early twentieth century. While flea markets today still include an abundance of second-hand goods, vastly improved living conditions in cities have pretty much eliminated the need to worry about actual fleas. That said, it's not a bad idea to launder any second-hand clothing or linens you buy before you use them.

Most Americans feel uncomfortable about haggling over prices. We accept the price we're given—it's part of our culture. In fact, even when it's expected for us to do so, as with buying cars and houses, we still feel awkward. This is probably due to our lack of practicing the art, which many countries have mastered by way of street bazaars and marketplaces. Instead, we tend to practice the art of *giving money away* at casinos in Las Vegas and Atlantic City!

It's a misconception to think that only big-ticket items should be negotiated. Keep in mind that every time you see a price tag, it can be changed. While you'll have a difficult time getting a price reduction in major retail stores, such as Macy's or Old Navy, there are plenty of places for you to go and plenty of circumstances to take advantage of.

▶ Flea Markets and Yard Sales

Without a doubt, these are two of the best places to practice your negotiating skills. Wherever and whenever there's a flea market or yard sale, you can expect the area's most highly proficient dealmakers to flock to the site. And expect them early! Before the sun even has a chance to rise, bargain hunters are already at the doorstep, waiting for vendors to bring out their goods. The reason for this is because the best selection is available first thing in morning when no one has had a chance to pick through items or buy them in bulk. Another reason these buyers show up early is because they usually have a full day of flea markets, yard sales, estate sales, and other sites to visit so they try to get to each place as early as possible.

When you're ready to enter the world of extreme bargaining, arrive at your destination early to get the best experience. Once inside, pick one of the early birds to "shadow." Discreetly follow this expert from vendor to vendor, observing the exchanges that are made. Listen to the negotiations. Make note of this person's voice inflections, body language, and tactics. How much time does the haggler spend talking with the vendor before starting to discuss price? What about negotiating style? What is the vendor's style? Are they friendly toward each other, or are the conversations strictly business? Are the results of their negotiation fair?

After you've observed a few haggling strategies, it's time to check out the vendors themselves. Here are a few tips:

- **Pay attention to how the vendor interacts with potential customers.** If she's pleasant, you can probably get a fair price from her. If she has a defensive attitude and isn't friendly, you might want to try your luck with another vendor.

- **Notice whether the vendor is willing to negotiate or if she turns a lot of people away.** Chances are that if she almost never comes down on price, you probably won't be able to practice your skills with her. You might want to check back with her toward the end of the day when she's eager to get as many sales as possible.

- **Determine how well the vendor knows her products by listening to her answers to shoppers' questions.** If she seems uncomfortable giving information, she probably doesn't know that much. Usually, if a person doesn't know the details about what she's selling, she won't negotiate with you because she doesn't want to get ripped off.

- **When buying more than a few items from one vendor, ask for a discount.** If you're unable to talk down the prices of the items you want to buy, try getting 10 to 15 percent off the total sale. If a vendor senses that she's about to lose a big sale, she'll more than likely find a way to compensate you.

- **Compare prices from one vendor to the next on similar items.** Most flea markets feature vendors that sell the same products; for instance, there could be five different booths selling computer software. Negotiate with each vendor, but don't buy right away. If one vendor says she'll sell you something for $40, use that as leverage for when you negotiate with the next vendor.

▶ **eBay**

To get in some extra practice, visit *www.ebay.com* and start bargaining with other Internet users for anything that piques your interest. You can find virtually anything from antique dolls to themed lunchboxes up for sale on this site. It's also a great way to get rid of some clutter if you have items to sell. You can guarantee that someone out there would give his left foot to have one of the items you've stored in a box labeled "junk."

Here's how eBay works. You search for an item by keyword or category. Look at the asking price, see what other people have **bid** on the item, and make your own bid. A date is posted telling when the auction will close, and you receive notification via e-mail if you win the bid. If you've never been on this website before, read the easy-to-follow instructions on the homepage and start bidding away.

BID: To bid is to offer a certain price for an item. This term is commonly used in the auction arena—another great place to get some practice in the art of negotiating. The only difference between this and, say, a flea market, is that in an auction, you're placing your bid through an auctioneer, who is a middleman between the seller and buyer.

Go Out to Eat

Dining out at a restaurant offers plentiful opportunities to test your negotiation know-how. Why? Because it's all about asking—and paying—for what you want. Employees are usually eager to please because they want a good tip; the kitchen staff wants to uphold its reputation for serving good food; and the management wants more people to go to the restaurant, so they count on their customers spreading the word about how great it was.

▶ Be Seated

When you get to the restaurant, ask the host or hostess for a specific table. If it's really busy, you probably won't be accommodated, but it certainly doesn't hurt to ask, especially when you're in negotiation training. Some other specifics you can ask for include the following:

- Being seated away from the entrance, kitchen, and restrooms
- Being seated at a booth instead of a table
- Being seated outdoors instead of indoors
- Being seated next to a window
- Being seated in a corner for privacy

Getting these concessions may seem like small successes, but the feeling you get after having your request fulfilled is a positive one.

▶ May I Take Your Order?

When your server comes to take your order, ask for something that's not on the menu. You can give any reason you like (you're in the mood for something else, you don't like the menu choices, or you're on a special diet), as long as you don't give up. If the server says "no" right off the bat, gather your things as if you're going to leave. At that point, she'll realize she's about to lose her tip and will probably tell you that she'll talk to the manager about it to see what she can do.

Another thing you can do is ask for a substitution. If an entrée comes with a side of fries but you'd prefer a salad instead, ask the server if he can make that change for you. He might say yes right off the bat, or he might tell you he can make the substitution but only for an additional $2.00 charge. If you're okay with that, great. If not, see if you can get him to waive the extra fee.

▶ Check, Please

Last but not least, paying for the meal is something that should always be negotiated if you had a bad experience in one area of service. If your server took your order incorrectly, forgot to bring you drinks, or served your food cold, these are all reasons for getting a discount off the total bill. If the meat you ordered was bad, the soda you received was flat, or if there was a hair somewhere on the plate, those items should come off the bill and you should get a discount on the total.

If you order something on the menu and the server comes back to tell you that they're out of that item, ask for a discount on what you choose to replace it with. This shows that you're still willing to have a meal at the restaurant even though what you want isn't available. If the establishment can't compensate you for your trouble, then why should you ever come back? Once you start to leave, the server will get the manager, who is sure to do whatever it takes to make you happy. Any restaurant manager would rather have 85 percent of the price of the meal than nothing at all.

Practice at Work

You can try out your new skills at the office in a variety of ways. Each of the following activities will give you the opportunity to practice the various stages of negotiating:

- **Planning**: Volunteer to be the designated party planner for birthdays, baby showers, and happy hours. Goals can include deciding on what type of party to have (breakfast get-together, luncheon, after-work appetizers), what kind of food to bring, and how to decorate for the theme.
- **Research**: For birthday parties, you'll want to do some investigating about the person whose birthday it is so you can create a theme around her interests and avoid including something she dislikes. For happy hours, find a few different places near the office and visit them to see what kinds of diversions (pool tables, dart boards, big-screen televisions), food specials (two-for-one appetizers, party platters), and drink specials they have.

- **Finding common ground**: Get a feel for what kind of food and snacks the majority likes, as well as input on where people would like to have the next celebration. If you work in an office where most people don't drink alcohol, you'll need to find a place for happy hour that's appropriate for their needs.
- **Coming up with alternatives**: Create a list of ideas and pass it around the office so people can add to it. This gets everyone involved and keeps things interesting.
- **Creating agendas**: Everyone's schedule is different, so coordinating them will be challenging. There will always be a few people who can't show up, so choose a date that fits into the majority's schedules.

Once you've gained confidence with a few of these more trivial at-work situations, you might feel ready to try the following big workplace negotiations.

▶ Asking for a Raise

It's always difficult to ask for a raise—for one thing, you might be afraid you'll get fired just for asking. You might feel that if you really do a great job, your boss should come to you with a pay increase, not the other way around. But it's simply not in your boss's best interest to give you a raise unless you ask for it. Luckily, there's a way to approach the subject without having to fear immediate termination. It begins with the realization that your boss isn't always aware of the great job you're doing.

Before you approach your boss, do some salary-comparison research, and reassess your benefits package. Then make a list of all your achievements and produce hard evidence that shows how your work has made an impact on the company. Gather any documentation of positive feedback you've received from superiors and peers in other departments as well as your own. Also, be prepared to counter any flaws, such as days you were late or left early, mistakes that were made, and so on. Don't get defensive or upset. Your boss knows that nobody's perfect, and she might just be looking for an explanation.

When you're ready to meet with your boss, **choose an appropriate time to discuss the issue**, such as during your performance review or at a scheduled time and place. Don't knock on your boss's door and expect a meeting right then and there. Also, don't approach him during the company's busy season when he is likely to be working hard and probably crunched for time.

▶ New Job Salary Negotiation

If you're interviewing for a new job, you must be prepared to negotiate a salary. First, find out if the person you'll be interviewing with is a supervisor, director, or vice president. This will determine what types of decisions the interviewer is allowed to make. Next, highlight all the skills that advanced you further in your previous jobs, including those that reflect your ability to learn fast. Estimate timeframes for your achievements to show how quickly you can **adapt** to the position.

ADAPT: To adapt is to adjust according to changing conditions. The ability to adapt is an important one to have in negotiations, as circumstances can change on a dime, and losing your cool might result in losing a deal.

When it's finally time to discuss salary, get a number before you give one (even just a range or an estimate). Never be the first to make an offer. The reason for this is twofold. If your offer is too high, you could be overlooked because other candidates produced a lower number for the employer to negotiate with. If your offer is too low, you'll get taken advantage of.

Then counter the offer by giving your range, *not* a single number. Use the high number of their range as the low number of your range and try to get a little above that number if possible. As mentioned previously, use benefits and perks as compensation for not getting the exact number you want. Can you negotiate an extra day off per month, a few extra personal days, and a sign-on bonus?

Remember, salary isn't the most important aspect of acquiring a new position. Look at the whole picture, and adjust each element as needed to get the best deal possible. Then compare the package with what other companies are offering to determine how well you'll fare.

Practice at Home

While you shouldn't go around negotiating with your spouse and children just for the fun of it, **household negotiations can be great practice for deal-making outside the home**. Since personal relations involve emotions that most business dealings don't, you'll have an extra challenge to work through when negotiating with your loved ones. The following are a couple of common areas of negotiation at home.

► Chores

From laundry to taking out the garbage, when it comes to household chores, there's something for everyone! However, chances are that you all have preferences. Cleaning the toilet grosses out your daughter, and your son can't seem to remember to separate the whites and the colors. Perhaps you dislike taking out the garbage, and your spouse hates dishpan hands. Have the whole family sit down at the table with a piece of paper and a pen to hash it out. You can either create a chart of chores with places to insert family members' names, or, if no one can agree, you can write each chore on a different slip of paper and take turns pulling them out of a hat. If you're not happy with the chore you get, you can trade with someone else.

► Clicker Control

Many households only have one television or computer in the house. In that case, you'll have to find a way to negotiate who gets to use these items when. Start by comparing schedules. If you like to watch games during baseball season, and your son has a favorite show that's on at the same time, take turns recording your programs so that you each have an equal chance to watch in real time. Similarly, if your kids need the computer for homework in the evenings and you work from home, do your best to finish your tasks before they get home from school. Also take into account the level of importance of the activity. If your son wants to watch the TV because he's bored but your daughter needs to watch a specific news program for a class assignment, try to facilitate an agreement in which your daughter uses the TV first, and your son watches what he wants when her news program is over.

Key Words in This Chapter

* Hypothetical
* Devil's advocate
* Flea market
* Bid
* Adapt

Key Phrases in This Chapter

* A great way to deliver your opening proposal is in speech form.
* Pay attention to how the vendor interacts with potential customers.
* Notice whether the vendor is willing to negotiate or if she turns a lot of people away.
* Determine how well the vendor knows her products by listening to her answers to shoppers' questions.
* When buying more than a few items from one vendor, ask for a discount.
* Compare prices from one vendor to the next on similar items.
* Choose an appropriate time to discuss the issue.
* Household negotiations can be great practice for deal-making outside the home.

Case Study—Some Conversations at the Flea Market

Imagine spending a Saturday afternoon at your local flea market or at a yard sale. All around you, negotiations are going on, hot and heavy. The conversations you overhear probably go something like one of these.

▶ **Poodles for Sale!**

Mr. Yardsale: How much is this pair of china poodles?

Ms. Fleamarketer: Aren't they nice? They're $10 each. I really love those little guys!

Mr. Yardsale: Yeah, they're nice, but that's a bit much, isn't it? Look, this one's got a chip in its tail.

Ms. Fleamarketer: Well, that's true. But these are antiques, from 1902. There's the maker's mark on the bottom there.

Mr. Yardsale: I don't know. Twenty dollars seems like a lot . . .

Ms. Fleamarketer: Well, I could sell you the pair for a discount. Say $18.00.

Mr. Yardsale: Call it $15 and you've got yourself a deal.

Ms. Fleamarketer: Done! I'm glad to know they're going to a good home.

Some things to notice:

1. The vendor seems to know something about what she's selling. That means she's more likely to negotiate with you.
2. The seller's not wedded to a single price. She offers to discount for a sale of the pair of objects. Most people are open to a similar arrangement if it means they're going to sell more than one of something.
3. The vendor's not unreasonable; she accepts that there's a chip on the tail of the one dog, but she argues that this is countered by the fact that they're antiques.

▶ **Get Your Furniture Here!**

Ms. Earlybird: I was admiring that chair over there with the embroidered pattern on the seat. What can you tell me about it?

Ms. Fleamarketer: You have a good eye. That's an interesting piece. It's early American, dating from 1812. If we turn it over here, you can see that the maker has carved his mark onto the bottom of the seat. I got this in last week as part of a consignment from an estate sale in another part of the state.

Ms. Earlybird: It seems to need some refurbishing. I can see that the one leg here is cracked, so that'll have to be repaired.

Ms. Fleamarketer: Yes, but don't do it yourself. Take it to a professional restorer. You don't want to damage the value of the piece, and a professional can tell you exactly how to go about repairing it.

Ms. Earlybird: I see you're asking $250. That seems like a lot.

Ms. Fleamarketer: Well, that takes into account the antiquity of the piece. And as you can see, even with that crack it's still in very good condition. The varnish has been very well preserved, and the wood has a lovely patina. And the embroidered seat is in very nice shape.

Ms. Earlybird: Would you be willing to discount if I bought more than one chair? I see that you have a set of four.

Ms. Fleamarketer: Certainly. If you purchase all four, I could go to $900.

Ms. Earlybird: That's only saving me $100. What if we said $750 for all four?

Ms. Fleamarketer: How about $800? That takes $200 off the price. I can also take $10 off our normal $40 delivery charge.

Ms. Earlybird: That sounds fine. I'm looking forward to seeing these in my dining room.

Ms. Earlybird has made a good deal for some nice pieces of furniture that are likely to appreciate in value—a point to keep in mind when making any purchase. We should also note:

1. Ms. Fleamarketer has displayed substantial knowledge about the piece, which should give Ms. Earlybird confidence in the value of what she's buying.
2. Ms. Earlybird asks for, and Ms. Fleamarketer agrees to, a discount for quantity. Most sellers will be happy to make some discount for a buyer who wants to purchase in bulk. In this case, Ms. Fleamarketer is even willing to knock $10 off the delivery price, making this a worthwhile bargain.
3. Like all good negotiators, Ms. Fleamarketer and Ms. Earlybird circle around the price before finally meeting in the middle.

► I Got Your Watches! Watches for Sale!

Mr. Bargainhunter: That's a nice-looking pocket watch back there—the one toward the top of the cabinet. What can you tell me about it?

Mr. Watchman: Sure. Uh, that's, uh, a genuine . . . watch from a long time ago. See, it's uh, got a lotta stuff engraved here on the inside. So it's, uh, valuable because of that.

Mr. Bargainhunter: Can you tell me where it came from?

Mr. Watchman: I think it came from some stuff I bought a couple of weeks ago. I don't remember exactly. I could probably check if you really need to know.

Mr. Bargainhunter: That won't be necessary. Does it run?

Mr. Watchman: Sure. I think it runs.

Mr. Bargainhunter: It doesn't seem to be running now.

Mr. Watchman: That's because it hasn't been wound up, you know what I'm saying? If you, uh, wound it up, it'd probably run fine.

Mr. Bargainhunter: Can you wind it for me so I can see if it runs?

Mr. Watchman: Not unless you're going to buy it. Are you going to buy it?

Mr. Bargainhunter: What's the asking price on it?

Mr. Watchman: Fifty dollars.

Mr. Bargainhunter: That seems like a lot, especially if there's a question of whether it runs. How about $30?

Mr. Watchman: Are you kidding me? For this watch? This is a bargain. I'm telling you, you won't find anything like that around here for this price. Fifty dollars is rock bottom.

Mr. Bargainhunter: Okay. Thanks very much, but I'll keep looking.

Mr. Watchman has done just about everything wrong, and it's not surprising that Mr. Bargainhunter decides to look elsewhere.

1. Mr. Watchman's pattern of speech, with all the uhs and ums, suggests a lack of confidence in what he's selling. If he's going to be successful, he'll have to work on eliminating these from his pitch.

2. Mr. Watchman doesn't seem to know much about the watch. In any negotiation, knowledge is power; whoever knows more usually gets the better end of the bargain.

3. Mr. Bargainhunter, quite reasonably, wants to know if the watch works before he pays money for it. The fact that Mr. Watchman isn't willing to meet this simple request saps Mr. Bargainhunter's confidence that he's been honestly dealt with.

4. Mr. Watchman is engaged in positional negotiating, unwilling to move from his price. The result, not surprisingly, is no sale.

Part III

Common Negotiations

Chapter 9

Buying a Home

THERE ARE LOTS OF negotiations involved in buying a home. You need to secure a good mortgage and agree with your family members on the location and type of housing you're looking for. Once you find the home you want to buy, the real negotiations will begin. You don't simply pay what the seller is asking. Using your negotiating skills, you'll be able to work out a price that both works for you and is acceptable to the seller.

The Real Estate Market

Once you've decided that you want to buy a house, the first step is to see what's out there. Drive around the neighborhoods you're interested in, keeping an eye out for For Sale signs. Check your local paper for upcoming open houses you can attend. Once you've found a house that you're interested in, the real work begins.

▶ Determine "Fair Price"

Before you can make an offer, you must determine a **fair price** for the home you want. Technically, this cannot be established until a property is actually sold, but in the meantime, you can estimate. Compare the property you want to buy with similar properties that have been sold in the area during the past year. This will give you a good idea of what the home you have your eye on is worth.

FAIR PRICE: This is defined as the highest price a ready, willing, and able buyer will pay and the lowest a ready, willing, and able seller will accept. You might also hear this referred to as "fair market value."

When you are ready to start negotiating, ask your realty agent to show you **comparables**. The term "comparables," in a real-estate setting, refers to the listing sheets that agents have describing properties that have recently been sold. Those sheets will contain all the pertinent information on the property, including the original asking price, all price reductions, the actual selling price, the date of the closing, and the date of the original listing contract. You can use the date of the original listing to determine how long the house was on the market before it sold.

Almost every real-estate office that belongs to a multiple-listing organization will have a comparables file or a digitized comparables database. Even independent agencies that do not share listings will keep a file of properties sold by their own offices and agents. The single-office file works well in large cities where many brokers are independents and tend to work only in tightly defined neighborhoods rather than trying to cover the entire city. It also works well in condo or co-op sales, where one or two real-estate agencies usually handle all the sales within a particular building.

After you have seen comparables, make a list of selling prices and addresses of the properties that you consider similar to the house you want. Take home photocopies of those listing sheets, if the agent is willing and allowed to give them to you. Compare and rate each property against the house you want to make an offer on.

▶ Compare Your "Fair Price" to the Seller's Price

Once you have determined what you think is a fair selling price for the property, compare it with what the seller is asking. If your evaluation price is higher than the asking price (a rare occurrence), do not get out your pen to sign an offer. Look again at the property, the neighborhood, the location, the lot, the time on the market, local conditions—everything. You may have missed something very important. However, if everything checks out, then act quickly. The seller may just have underpriced his property; so, buy before word gets out and another buyer appears and starts a bidding war.

It is much more likely that the asking price will be more than your estimate of fair market value. That is what negotiating is all about. Put yourself in the seller's shoes for a moment. Why do you think he set the price so high? To allow room for negotiating? Because he has installed new carpeting? He wants to be repaid for their newly remodeled $14,000 kitchen? Take the position that the amenities or upgrades do not always add to the resale value of a home.

Figure out your ideal price for the home (likely to be a "steal" price), your estimate of fair market value, and your absolute "top-dollar" price. Why would you want to pay a top-dollar price that is higher than the fair market value of the property? Because until the contract is signed, the fair market value is still a guess, and even professional real-estate appraisers can differ in their fair market value estimates. Therefore, you must leave yourself a **margin of error**, a realistic dollar space that will keep you from becoming too rigid during the negotiations.

MARGIN OF ERROR: A margin of error is an allowance for miscalculation or change in circumstances. This is helpful in many negotiations but particularly in real estate. If you misjudge the market or have a sudden change in your finances, you'll be prepared to roll with the punches.

Most important of all during this negotiating stage is that you do not tell your real-estate agent your "steal" figure or your "top-dollar figure." Remember, the agent represents the seller. If you tell the agent that you are willing to go up to as high as $123,000 for a house listed at $125,000, then $123,000 is probably what you will end up paying. You have to play your hand close to the vest during the negotiating process, even with your agent.

▶ **Consider the Market at the Moment**

Besides checking comparables and working the numbers, **it is important that you gauge the state of the market in your area at the time you want to buy**. For example, if it is a hot sellers' market, where properties are moving quickly, and the home you want is a desirable one with potentially wide market appeal, start your negotiations fairly close to market value. You do not want to lose the property playing games over price.

In some situations, although this is uncommon, a house or a location is so "hot" that simultaneous offers are made. Sometimes the best of these is simply accepted, with no negotiating. More often the seller negotiates with all prospective buyers simultaneously. They are "out for the kill." If you truly want that property in such a situation, here are some tactics that will help:

- Offer your best price, but be willing to move up another $500 or $1,000. Do not, however, get caught up in auction fever and bid the house up far above its market value.
- Ask for as few extras in the sale as possible.
- Make the closing date as agreeable to the seller as you can.
- Have loan approval from a mortgage lender.

On the other hand, if the market is soft where you are looking (sometimes called a buyers' market), if the seller is under need-to-sell stress, or if the house is not particularly appealing to most people— they cannot see the potential that you can, or their needs are different from yours—you can move more slowly and negotiate over a wider range. In these situations, it is possible to get a much better deal with a bit of patience and perseverance.

Offers and Counteroffers

You may hear people say that 10 percent below asking price is a good first offer. It isn't, really. There is no one "good" initial offer based upon asking price. Why? Because there are so many variables in real estate and because sellers rarely set their asking prices with consideration to market value or other rational thought processes. They want to get the most they can for their properties, and many have emotional ties to their homes. Would you offer 10 percent less than the asking price of a home that is overpriced by $25,000 or more?

Each and every piece of real estate is unique, and so is each selling situation. So, you can understand why generic rules of thumb in real estate are dangerous. But if you must have a guideline, a first offer that is 10 percent below your fair market value estimate—not the seller's asking price—will keep you from insulting the seller. It will also keep you from having your first offer snapped up because it was more than the seller thought he would actually get for the property.

► Making the Offer

Your offer cannot just be verbal. Most residential sales agents will refuse to present a verbal offer to the seller that is not accompanied by an **earnest money** check and specific information on financing, closing date, and other details of the sale. A buyer cannot call an agent and say, "Ask them if they'll take $139,500." That buyer could be asking the same question of four different agents about four different properties, a situation that can end up presenting serious problems. Your offer must be presented to the seller in writing.

EARNEST MONEY: Earnest money is a sum of money that you provide along with your offer that demonstrates to the seller the seriousness of your intent to buy. Think of it like a deposit.

When your real-estate agent hears the word *offer,* he or she might whip out a binder, a short form that includes your name and address, a few lines about the property being bid on, and the amount of your earnest money deposit (usually $500 or $1,000). If you are handed a binder, be certain it contains the clause "subject to review by the buyer's attorney within five business days." That will allow you to have your lawyer look over the form (and will also allow you an out if you change your mind about that property).

Most agents will want you to sign a contract before they present your offer to the seller. If you sign the contract, and if the seller agrees to your offer and also signs that form, you have bought the house.

▶ The Counteroffer

The counteroffer is the seller's response to your initial bid. Sometimes it names the actual amount they want for the property, but not usually. Most sellers still have some room in their first-response prices, even when they say, "Not a penny less." You now must work toward a meeting of the minds.

In a journal or notebook, record your first offer, its terms, and its contingencies (or have your agent give you a copy of the offer form after it is completely filled out and signed). When you get the counteroffer, record not only its facts and figures but also what the agent says the seller said. Does he want a quick closing? Is this his bottom price? Is he anxious to sell? However, do not take a word of what you hear as gospel truth. In negotiating, you must always keep testing for what is "real" and what is just a negotiation tactic. The counteroffer is usually returned to you on your original offer form, with numbers crossed out and new numbers written in and initialed.

▶ Your Second and Third Offers

Your second offer should not be your top dollar, but it should be closer to your estimate of the market value. Have the agent write out a whole new offer form. Do not work with scratched-out figures and initials on the original sheet, since this will only create confusion.

Add to your negotiating journal the facts of this second offer and any asides that are mentioned by anyone. Keeping such a written account of who said what and when may prevent arguments, misunderstandings, and denials later. It will also give you a chance to review what happened throughout the process.

At each step of the bidding, it is worth mentioning to your real-estate agent the flaws of the house—something to the effect that of course you like and want the house, but it does need kitchen remodeling, or you really wanted a two-car, not a one-car, garage. You want your agent to know—and relay to the seller—that you are not so committed to this house that you will pay anything to own it. There are other homes out there that could suit you, too. Even though you may feel this is the perfect house for you, if the seller knows that, they will have the upper hand in the negotiating, and you are likely to pay a higher price for it.

Most homes are sold upon or before the buyer's third offer. Sometimes, however, the negotiating goes on for many days. The procedure is always the same—offer, counteroffer. You and the seller are making adjustments, circling around each other, and trying to find a place to meet. Here is where the advice of a good realty agent can be invaluable.

The Emotions of House Hunting

Getting emotional—whether the emotion is on the buyer's or seller's side—can heat up the negotiating process to the point where the real-estate agent wants to run for cover! This is not good. **Acting rationally is essential when you are negotiating to buy a home.** Here are the most common emotions that carry away both buyers and sellers.

▶ Love

For you, this means love of the house you are negotiating for, but you should try not to fall head over heels for it. If you start thinking that this is the only house for you and that you will never find another house as good anywhere, you might as well forget about negotiating effectively. Try to remember there are other houses that will suit you just as well—and maybe better—even if you haven't found them yet.

If you lose the house you love, and you have the luxury of time, it is a good idea to wait a while before going out house-hunting again. You do not want to buy on the rebound if you can avoid it. Purchasing the wrong house is a costly mistake.

▶ Anger

This emotion makes an appearance in most real-estate negotiations at some point or another. The buyer may get angry at the seller, the seller may get angry at the buyer, they both can get angry at the real-estate agent, and the agent can get angry at them. Buying a house can be stressful, and no one wants to be taken advantage of.

It might be hard to stay calm and rational, but that should be your mantra during the negotiating process. Here are some suggestions for doing just that:

- **Take time to cool off.** If you feel your frustration building to an unmanageable level, say, "I'd like to take some time to think about this before continuing." Hang up the phone, leave the room, or go take a walk around the block.
- **Define the cause of your anger.** People sometimes find themselves furious without knowing why. Ask yourself, "What got this started?" Once you answer that question, it is easier to say, "How can I settle this?"
- **Stick to the point.** If you are negotiating over a closing date, do not let the issue of who is going to fix the broken toilet take over the discussion.
- **Don't burn bridges.** It is hard to come back from "Take your stupid house and stuff it." Avoid accusing the other party. "This is all your fault" gets you nowhere. Ask instead, "How did we get to this point, and where should we go from here?"
- **Don't lie.** If you said something yesterday and changed your mind overnight, say so. Do not deny what you said. Do not fib about your financial situation—you will be found out anyway.

Conveniently "forgetting" something counts as a lie here, too. Nothing sours a deal faster than contradictions about money.

▶ **Possessiveness and Greed**

Sometimes it is difficult for sellers to part emotionally with their property. Some fight to keep every stick that is not nailed down, and they expect to be paid dearly for every one that is. That could be seen as possessiveness.

When people buy, however, they want the most for their money. "That should go with the house" is the usual attitude, since they are anticipating the out-of-pocket expenses for everything that does not go with the house. That could be seen as greed. There is no right answer here. If you get into an argument over bits and pieces, ask yourself if possessiveness and/or greed are factors. Sometimes just recognizing those feelings helps to resolve the issue.

For Sale by Owner

When you're dealing with homes that are "for sale by owner" (or FSBOs), no real-estate agent is involved in the negotiations. The same principles for negotiating apply, but there is, of course, no middle man. That said, you'll want to get a lawyer to help with a "for sale by owner" deal. You should always have a lawyer in a case where there is no real-estate agent involved, but do not use the same legal counsel the sellers use.

How do you begin the negotiations? After your second visit to the home you like (the visit where you explored the house more thoroughly than you did on your initial visit), wait a day or two before making an offer. The purpose of this is to heighten the sellers' anticipation and to make your offer sound well-thought out.

To determine fair market value, go through computer printout sheets you have secured from real-estate agents for similar properties in the neighborhood. The bargaining process is similar in this case to bargaining through a real-estate agent, but sitting down face-to-face with sellers is always difficult. Keep rational and friendly, and remember that your primary tool for acceptance is that fair market value. Your offer hands them a quick sale, no more disruption in having a house on the market, and no sales **commission** to pay.

Still, they probably will not accept your first price. So, back you come with a second bid. That should usually be the fair market value minus the usual real-estate commission in the area (probably 6 or 7 percent). Of course, the sellers aren't using an agent, so there is no commission to be paid here.

COMMISSION: A commission is a sum or percentage allowed to agents, sales representatives, etc., for their services. In the case of a FSBO, there are no agents to pay, so commissions don't come into play.

In the best possible scenario, the buyer and seller will split the amount of the real-estate commission and set the selling price between market value and the price the owner would have netted after paying an agent's commission (if they had used one). All of the extras, such as closing dates and financing, can be worked out then and there, or with the attorneys for both sides present. The attorneys will draw up the contract to buy.

That's how a neat, tidy sale works. But life does not always follow such a script. The sellers may be new to this business and hold out high hopes for a top-dollar price. When you come up against a stone wall, do not beat your head against it, no matter how much you like the house. Write down your best offer, with your name, address, and phone number, and leave it with the sellers. Tell them to call you if they change their mind, and then continue house-hunting. You might want to keep in touch with them from time to time to ask how they are doing.

Do not make another offer, but if they do come down a little, perhaps you will be willing to go up a little. This is how negotiating works.

Also, you should never give an earnest money deposit directly to the sellers. That check should be handed to your lawyer.

The Closing

Use the closing date in your negotiations. Time is money, so the saying goes. **In negotiating for a home, time can be worth money if you use it as a tool.** Try to find out early in the game what the sellers want out of the sale in terms of time as well as in terms of price. Do they need a quick **closing** because they are carrying two mortgages? Do they need time to find another house? Do they need flexibility in a closing date because they are having a house built and do not know exactly when it will be completed?

CLOSING: The closing is the date when the title of the property is actually transferred from the seller to the buyer. This date can be a valuable tool in negotiating to buy a house.

With your original low offer, you will be asked to name a closing date. If it works for you, name one that is not likely to be to the sellers' liking. If they need a quick closing, set your offer date for three or four months in the future. If they want a distant closing, ask for one in four to six weeks. Then, as you respond to their counteroffers, you can increase the bid by very little cash but sweeten the deal by moving the proposed closing date into line with the sellers' needs. It is almost always worth money.

Key Words in This Chapter
- Fair price
- Comparables
- Margin of error
- Earnest money
- Commission
- Closing

Key Phrases in This Chapter

- It is important that you gauge the state of the market in your area at the time you want to buy.
- Each and every piece of real estate is unique, and so is each selling situation.
- Acting rationally is essential when you are negotiating to buy a home.
- Sometimes it is difficult for sellers to part emotionally with their property.
- In negotiating for a home, time can be worth money if you use it as a tool.

Case Study—Real Estate Negotiating

Imagine that you want to buy a house. You know what you want and what you need. You've looked at a seemingly endless succession of properties and found one that suits you. Now you sit down with your realtor, Ms. Happyhomes, and determine how your negotiation is going to go.

Ms. Houseache: Well, I think I've seen something I like very much, Ms. Happyhomes. That last property we looked at was what I'm looking for.

Ms. Happyhomes: I'm very glad. It'll be great to settle in a new home and really call it your own. So let's put together an offer on the property.

Ms. Houseache: Great! What do we need to do?

Ms. Happyhomes: I have all your basic information on file, so we can enter that into the computer and print out the form for the offer. But before we name a price, we need to decide on the property's **fair market value**.

Ms. Houseache: Well, the property's listed on the market at $275,000.

Ms. Happyhomes: Yes, but that may not actually be what it's worth. The homeowner is certainly trying to get the most he can for it. Let's see what it was assessed at. According to the county records, the property was assessed a year ago at $265,000.

Ms. Houseache: So is that what we should offer?

Ms. Happyhomes: Not necessarily, because property values in the area may have increased since then. Or they may have decreased. We should look at what comparable properties in the area are selling at as well. That'll give us an idea of what range of offer we should consider making. **We also need to look at the state of the market in this neighborhood.** Are people buying houses in this area? If they aren't, why not?

Now, look. We have three houses sold on that street in the past year. These two have roughly the same square footage as the one you're interested in, but one sold for $259,000, and the other sold for $268,000. Of course, the second one also has a fireplace and an extra half bath, so that would potentially increase the price.

Ms. Houseache: Well, the house I want has that built-in brick grill in the backyard. And it's got a lot of extra closet space.

Ms. Happyhomes: Exactly. Those might be contributing factors to the high asking price. But the seller also wants **some room to come down.** So we need to figure out an offer that's going to be serious but reflects the house's fair market price. Now, what about extras?

Ms. Houseache: What do you mean?

Ms. Happyhomes: Well, is there anything you saw in the house when we were going through it that you'd like to ask the seller about leaving? For instance, I saw you looking at the washer and dryer.

Ms. Houseache: Yes. I don't have a washer and dryer, so it would be great if we could get him to leave those for me. I also liked the curtains in the living room—they really suit that room well. Could we ask about those?

Ms. Happyhomes: Sure. We can ask about anything. But remember that the more things you say you want, the more leverage he has to ask things of you.

Ms. Houseache: What kinds of things would he ask for? I mean, apart from more money?

Ms. Happyhomes: Oh, lots of things. He would ask that the closing date be arranged to suit his convenience, not yours. Or he could ask that you pay some of his closing costs. There are some things we're going to ask him to do to the house, and he might try to negotiate on some of those.

Ms. Houseache: What kinds of things would we be asking him to do?

Ms. Happyhomes: Well, the house is on a septic system, so we should ask when it was last serviced. If it's been a while, we'll ask him to have it taken care of before the closing. We should also ask about the roof. It looked a bit old to me, and we might need to ask him to replace or repair it. There was also some exposed wiring in the basement, and you should ask that it be covered up.

Ms. Houseache: Yes, and one of the upstairs windows had a crack in it. I'd like that to be fixed.

Ms. Happyhomes: Good. Make a list of everything you want him to do to the house before you move in, and we'll ask about them. After we have the property inspected, we may find some more things that we'll need to ask about, but for right now make your own list.

Ms. Houseache: So we come back to the issue of how much to offer initially for the house.

Ms. Happyhomes: Yes. I'd say a fair offer would be $263,000. That's quite a bit below the asking price, but it gives us room to come up, and it shows we're serious. If necessary, we can also give on some of these other issues, but you need to tell me which items on the list you're going to compile are absolutely essential to the deal and which are ones we can give away in return for other things.

Ms. Houseache: Okay. We'll offer $263,000. So now what happens? You send the offer to his realtor, and we wait to see what he says?

Ms. Happyhomes: Yes, but we have to accompany the offer with a check. It's called **earnest money**, and it shows that we're serious in our offer.

Ms. Houseache: How much do we have to put up?

Ms. Happyhomes: You can write a check for $1,000. I'll put it in an escrow account, and if the sale doesn't go through for some reason, you'll get it back. If we go ahead with the sale, it'll be applied to the price of the house.

Ms. Houseache: Okay.

Ms. Happyhomes: Great. I'll draw up the paperwork, and we should hear back from the agent in about five business days.

This conversation isn't the actual negotiation that will happen via telephone and e-mail between Ms. Happyhomes and the realtor representing the seller. Rather, it's about the necessary preparation for negotiation. From this discussion we can see that:

1. The fair market price for a home is not the same as the asking price (it's probably below that). It's based on several factors including the last assessed value of the home, comparable prices of similar houses in the neighborhood, any special features the home contains, and, quite possibly, special features in the neighborhood itself (e.g., how good the school system is, presence of parks and other recreation areas, crime rate, etc.).

2. The buyer, Ms. Houseache, needs to have a clear list of requests going into the negotiation. She'll never have this much leverage again, since the seller wants to sell as soon as possible. She also needs to distinguish between wants and needs—what are the requests that are deal-breakers for her, and what could she live without.

3. The offer must be serious. There's no point in making an offer that's far below the asking price, unless Ms. Houseache and Ms. Happyhomes really believe the house is vastly overpriced. Even in that case, they're better off waiting for the price to come down over time, rather than make an offer that will be seen as insultingly low.

Chapter 10

Negotiating with Your Kids

YOUR CHILDREN ARE YOUR pride and joy— and the toughest negotiators you'll ever have to face! They're constantly trying your patience, pleading for your consent, and arguing to get their way. These day-to-day battles can be stressful, but most things can be worked out. And just like negotiations you take on in the professional world, it's essential that you keep your cool at home. This chapter is your quick reference guide for learning how to implement the steps of negotiation in your family's struggles.

Parenting Styles

Research shows there are three basic parenting styles: authoritarian, permissive, and democratic. These styles serve as guides for describing how parents deal with their children. While no parent fits into one style alone, it's important to look at these styles individually to understand how each one may be effective.

Your parenting skills are influenced in part by your own parents, other family members, and friends. And there's so much information available on good parenting, including books, magazines, and websites. But ultimately, the driving force behind your parenting style lies in your own personal belief system—your values, thoughts, ethics, feelings, and opinions.

▶ Authoritarian Ruler

This style is all about rule enforcement. Authoritarian parents want to be obeyed without question. They possess all of the control and rarely let children have a say in matters. They tell their children what to do, and the children listen. If they don't listen, they are met with consequences such as yelling, threatening, and punishment. Because this type of parent is so strict, children never learn how to think for themselves. They exist inside a world with little freedom to explore, make mistakes, or learn from those mistakes.

Authoritarian parents demand respect, which in turn causes children to fear their parents. As children get older, they're more likely to rebel as they begin enjoying the feeling of freedom they never really had.

▶ Permissive Coddler

In contrast to the authoritarian style, permissive parenting involves letting your children do whatever they want. Any rules that are made are broken time and time again because children know it can be done without any consequence. When children misbehave, the permissive parent will have a talk with them but won't enforce any punishment. Thus, children learn that they can get away with pretty much anything. Permissive parents risk raising spoiled children who are used to getting their way.

▶ Democratic Leader

Children raised in the democratic style are taught how to be responsible because they're given choices on how to solve issues. Their opinions and feelings matter and are taken into consideration when decisions are made. Parents set reasonable rules and discuss the need for these rules with their children as well as help them understand what the consequences are for breaking them. They also provide children with plenty of options for handling problems and always incorporate their ideas into the solution.

Because these children are given the freedom to think creatively, they grow up to be independent and confident in their ability to make sound decisions. Presenting them with choices in situations where they initially feel helpless builds their self-esteem and lets them feel like they contribute to the family.

Sibling Rivalry

Brothers and sisters were born to drive each other crazy! It seems like every time you turn around they're arguing over who gets to have the one toy out of hundreds that they both want to play with at that moment. You've tried everything—yelling, punishing, taking the toy away—but they end up in the same argument the very next day. One way to break this cycle is to **learn how you can teach your negotiating skills to your kids**. By using the steps of negotiation, you'll teach your children how to control their anger, calm down before the argument gets out of control, come up with solutions to the problems they are facing, and know when it's time to call in the mediators—Mom and Dad. With your guidance, they can learn how to work out their differences by giving each other the space and independence they so desperately crave.

▶ **Identify the Problem**

The first thing you need to do is stop the misbehaving. If one child is throwing toys or hitting the other, step in and make it clear that this is unacceptable behavior. Next, ask them to describe what the problem is. Since they'll both want to speak first, you'll need to call on one to go first and let the other one know he can go first next time. After each child explains his side of the story, repeat what each one said and ask if you understood it correctly. Once they agree with you, ask them, one at a time, if they understand the other one's problem.

You'll usually get a "Yeah, but . . ." answer to this question, so be ready to jump in and prevent any statements that will **antagonize** the other child. You're trying to teach them how to remain calm and deal with one issue at a time. By reiterating their problems individually, you're letting them know that you understand them and know what they want. Asking them to openly recognize the other sibling's problem gives them the opportunity to understand what happened to make everybody so upset.

ANTAGONIZE: To antagonize a person is to act in opposition to him, often just for the fun of it. This usually makes the other person feel hostile or resentful. Siblings antagonize each other constantly, and they rarely have a good reason for doing so. Nip this behavior in the bud and make it clear that it's unacceptable.

This first step is an important one because it teaches your children how to let go of the anger they feel for the other person in the argument. It also teaches them how to communicate effectively so others will understand them. Another thing they learn from this step is that you will always be willing to give them the floor and allow them to tell their own side of the story. Because they know you will listen to them, they will be more likely to come to you with problems.

▶ Find Solutions

Once the problems are out in the open, the next step is to actively engage the siblings in the process of coming up with solutions. Start off by giving your suggestion in the form of a "What if" question; then ask each child for an idea on how to fix the problem. Acknowledge their answers with positive statements like, "That's good" or "We can certainly give that a try" so they feel like they're not always giving the wrong answers. Keep exchanging ideas until all of you can agree on the best one and restate the final solution so both siblings are clear on what needs to happen. For example, "Jimmy will use the computer for one hour after school while Tommy does his homework, and then Tommy will use the computer for one hour after dinner while Jimmy does his homework."

▶ Establishing a Set of Rules

Depending on what the siblings are arguing over, **a set of rules will help prevent future disagreements about the same issue**. For example, if they're fighting over who gets to take the dog out for a walk before dinner, create a schedule in which they each get to do it every other day. If an argument gets violent, establish a rule in which both siblings will be punished no matter who hit first

In addition to setting rules, let your children know that they can always come to you when they're experiencing problems that they can't solve on their own. Eventually, they'll learn how to handle their own disputes and work out the issues for themselves.

Do Your Homework

The best negotiating skill you can apply here is setting an agenda and teaching your children how to stick to it. **Designate a specific time and place in the house for your children to do their homework every night.** The time right before or right after dinner is usually favored because they will have had plenty of time to unwind and play with friends after school. If necessary, meet with teachers ahead of time to find out the types of assignments being handed out and the average time that each student should expect to spend on homework.

Choose a place that's easy for your children to see you in case they have questions: the kitchen table or the desk in the study provide flat surfaces to write on and plenty of light. You can also give your children a few options or let them come up with some ideas of their own. If they suggest the picnic table outside, explain why this might not work (wind blows papers away, rain gets everything wet) and offer more choices. You also might want to busy yourself with your own work, such as paying bills or opening mail, so your children feel like you're all accomplishing tasks together.

If your children give you a hard time about doing their homework, offer to go through it with them, but make sure they know they have to do the work themselves. If they get distracted and start asking for snacks or toys, tell them you'll think about fixing a snack when the homework is finished, and provide something to drink instead.

One way to **motivate** your children to do their homework is to set up a workstation complete with all the school supplies they'll ever need: pencils, pens, markers, crayons, scissors, glue stick, stapler, and plenty of paper. If you have room, create a little area for them in the study so they feel they have their own space. However, monitor their work so they don't lose focus by playing with all the supplies you've put out for them.

MOTIVATE: In any negotiation, you need to find ways to motivate, or persuade, the other party to do what you want them to do. Kids especially need motivation when it comes to doing their homework or their chores. Note, though, that motivation is not the same as bribery!

Chores

Chores play an important and necessary role in your child's life. Doing chores teaches responsibility, builds self-esteem and self-reliance, and allows the child to feel important. Children are able to help at a very early age, and it should be encouraged as soon as they're capable. Otherwise, the older they are when you begin giving them chores, the harder it is to get them to cooperate.

Be sure you assign chores that are appropriate to your child's age. Young children love pitching in around the house because it makes them feel "all grown up" and proud of themselves for doing a great job. However, the older they get, the less eager they are about doing chores because they'd rather spend their time playing with toys or hanging out with friends.

▶ Be Creative with Preschoolers

Toddlers love to be called upon to do any task you throw their way. Their curious little minds are always looking for the next engaging activity and the next opportunity to show Mom and Dad how smart they are. For this reason, you can turn any small task into a big deal for your child. Reserve a little extra time in the morning, and ask your children if they can dress themselves that day. You can even let them choose their outfits, adding even more importance to the task.

At this age, children are also capable of picking up their own clothes and putting them in the laundry basket. Make the chore fun by taking a trip to the store with your child to pick a special basket just for this use. Bright colors and lovable animals always win children over.

You can teach organization skills by having children keep their books stacked neatly, their toys put away, and their beds made. Occasionally leave little surprises on the bookshelf, in the toy box, or under the pillow to encourage your child to continue doing the tasks.

▶ Use a Task Board for Grade-Schoolers

Since children who are in grade school have more responsibilities (homework, extracurricular activities), they're not as interested in taking out the trash, feeding the dog, or setting the table as they are in playing video games or riding their bikes. Because there's a lot to occupy their minds, they often forget to do chores or just brush them off as useless or boring. One way to keep your children focused on the importance of their duties at home is to set up a task board in a place where they'll be sure to see it, such as the kitchen. You can use the gold star system on a board you make yourself, or you can purchase one from a store. Your goal is to get them to check the schedule and perform the duties required of them for that day. Make sure you also write in your own chores so they can see how everyone in the family has a responsibility.

Alternatively, if your daughter loves math, you can challenge her with a question for each chore. For example, if her job is to take out the trash, ask her to measure the distance between the house and the garbage barrel.

▶ Be Specific with Teenagers

Teenagers can be difficult when it comes to doing chores. Because they're older, their responsibilities are more involved and more time-consuming. They don't want to spend an hour washing, drying, and folding the laundry or doing the dishes and vacuuming all the rugs in the house. They want to talk on the phone, go out with their friends, and shop at the mall.

The key to negotiating with your teens is to treat them like adults. Draw up a mock contract and explain how you're going to use it to bind the agreement that the two of you will make. Next, sit down to discuss and negotiate terms, concessions, and consequences of breaking the contract, settle on a final agreement, and create the official contract. Terms can include what chores the teen is responsible for, concessions can be what the teen will be allowed to do if the chore is completed, and consequences can include what privileges the teen will lose if the contract is broken. Adjust the contract as needed to fit your teenagers' lifestyle. For example, if they decide to take on more extracurricular activities or a part-time job, you'll need to come up with a new schedule that allows them to get their chores done as well.

Allowance

There are two schools of thought on allowance. Some believe that giving an allowance for chores weakens the importance of getting the chores done. If children believe that they should receive money every time they do something around the house, they'll be more likely to rebel against doing the chore and less likely to do things around the house without being asked or given money. On the other hand, a lot of parents believe that giving an allowance for chores provides children with an incentive for doing the work. **Ultimately, it's up to you to decide what works best for your family.**

▶ The Pros

Granting your child an allowance is a privilege that teaches them many valuable lessons that they will carry into their adult lives. It improves their math skills, teaches them responsibility and the value of saving money, and gives them a basic understanding of how the world works. It also teaches them how to prioritize their wants, set goals to acquire the things they want, and feel a sense of accomplishment when a goal is reached. Because there are so many things they want you to buy for them (toys, snacks, games), it's important to involve them in financial processes. Doing so helps them understand why you can't buy them everything their hearts desire. An allowance also serves as a useful negotiating tool when they're begging you to buy them "just this one thing and I won't ask for anything else ever again."

▶ Finance 101

When you make the decision to give children their own money, you also need to teach them how to use it. Explain to them where you get your money and how you **manage** it. Tell them what a budget is, and show them how you balance your checkbook or manage your finances online. You can explain it in simple terms that they'll understand and give them examples of how they can start using their money in some of the same ways. The sooner they begin to understand the concept, the sooner they'll understand how negotiating works.

MANAGE: To manage something is to take charge of or control it. Kids need to be taught the art of management in many arenas, from money to emotions, and the best way they can learn is by watching you exhibit the correct behavior.

Let's say there's a video game your daughter is really anxious to get, but it costs so much money that she wouldn't be able to get it until she saved her allowance for ten months. Use this opportunity to give her choices and explain the pros and cons of each one. If she borrowed the money from you, she'd have to go ten months without an allowance to pay you back. What if there were other things she wanted between now and then? How would she feel if her friends invited her to go for ice cream, but she didn't have the money to go? Give her the option of doing extra chores to earn a little more money. After you discuss different money concepts and provide various options, she may discover that the video game isn't as important as she thought.

Snack Time

Kids love snacks as much as they love toys. That said, it's just as important to teach them the benefits of good nutrition as it is to teach them how to use money wisely to get the things they want. To begin with, it's not always a good idea to use snacks as a means of rewarding your children. They'll have a hard time learning how to pay attention to their bodies and how to recognize when they're hungry as opposed to when they just want something sweet.

Another disadvantage to rewarding your children with snacks is that they will begin to associate emotion (happiness) with food, a dangerous thought process that, if not controlled, often leads to one of the nation's leading epidemics—obesity.

▶ **Make It Fun**

Your children learn from your cooking and eating habits, so the best way to teach them about eating healthy is to involve them in the preparation of food. When they ask you for a snack, invite them to look in the refrigerator with you and brainstorm ideas. Celery sticks with peanut butter make a crunchy, nutritious snack they can prepare themselves. A cup of their favorite yogurt with some granola or nuts sprinkled on top is a lot like an ice cream sundae but healthier. Another idea is to answer their request for a snack by giving them an art project. Choose colorful vegetables, fruits, cheeses, and nuts and show them how to make funny faces or pretty flowers with the ingredients. Make popcorn and experiment with a few different spices, such as cinnamon or cumin.

▶ **Let Them Help**

When it's time to prepare food, get your children involved. Let them handle the food and help choose the pans or bowls you'll need. Show them how to crack an egg and explain that eggs are laid by chickens. If someone in the family is on a diet, explain that by removing the yolk from the egg white you can decrease the amount of fat and cholesterol in the meal. Show them how you cook rice (explaining that the grains absorb the water), sauté vegetables, and bake a potato. If they're interested in science, they'll be fascinated by the chemistry involved in making yeast breads or pizza dough from scratch.

▶ **Don't Give In**

Your kids will have access to snacks at school and at their friends' houses that you may not keep in your house. They'll even be drawn in by captivating commercials they see on TV. Before long, they'll come home begging for these new fruit snacks or the latest juice drink. Don't **acquiesce**. As their parent, their health is in your hands. Explain that certain snacks and beverages are full of sugar, which can cause cavities and weaken their immune systems, causing them to get sick. Instead, offer to make a similar snack at home with natural ingredients. Look up recipes for fruit leather online, and squeeze fresh juice straight from the fruit in the morning. Kids will enjoy the process, and they'll realize the real thing often tastes just as good.

ACQUIESCE: To acquiesce is to give in or agree. In many negotiations it's smart to acquiesce after a certain amount of time; you both want to reach a deal, and someone has to budge to make it happen. It's different with your kids, though. You're the parent, and the rules and guidelines you create are meant to keep them healthy and safe.

Key Words in This Chapter

- Antagonize
- Motivate
- Manage
- Acquiesce

Key Phrases in This Chapter

- Learn how you can teach your negotiating skills to your kids.
- A set of rules will help prevent future disagreements about the same issue.
- Designate a specific time and place in the house for your children to do their homework every night.
- Chores play an important and necessary role in your child's life.
- Ultimately, it's up to you to decide what works best for your family.

Case Study—Who Gets the Car Tonight?

Negotiating with kids (let's face it) is a pain. Unlike business negotiations, children can veer off into irrationality at any moment. And talk about positional negotiators! The hardest thing in the world is to get a teenager to understand the value of win-win negotiating. Let's look at a typical scenario:

Sally: Mom! I need the car tonight.

Bob: Hey, wait a minute. I need it. I've got to go pick up some of the guys before the game and get pizza.

Sally: Well, I asked first. So I get it.

Bob: Yeah? Well, I'm older. So *I* get it.

Ms. Busymom: Look, you two, I'm getting sick of this. Every Friday night we have this same argument. Why can't you work something out between you?

Bob: What's to work out? I'm oldest, and that means I should get first dibs on the car.

Sally: Mom, that's totally unfair. If we do it that way, I'll never get to use the car on the weekend. He's *always* going somewhere with it.

Bob: Hey, it's not my fault if I've got a busy social life. I say oldest gets first pick.

Sally: Well, I say Mom should choose, because it's her car. Anyway, most of your friends have cars. None of mine do; I'm the only one. So I need it more than you. I say whoever needs it more gets it.

Bob: No way!

Ms. Busymom: Okay, that's it. We're going to work out a system for this. I'm not going to spend my weekends caught in between you two while you fight about the car.

Sally: What are you going to do?

Ms. Busymom: We're going to draw up a contract, and you two are going to sign it. I'll post it on the refrigerator, and if there's any argument, you can look at it and figure out how to resolve your disagreements.

Bob: You're kidding, right? A contract?

Ms. Busymom: All right, sit down. Now, Bob, how many days a week do you think you need the car?

Bob: Seven.

Ms. Busymom: Come on, now. Be serious. You're not going to get it seven days a week. How many days?

Bob: Well, I want it on Friday and Saturday nights so I can hang with the guys. And Tuesday night I go over to study with Gloria Hunnerford and Sandy, so I need it then.

Sally: Now, wait . . .

Ms. Busymom: Hold your horses, honey. You'll get to talk in a minute. Okay, Bob, that's three nights. Any others?

Bob: Thursday I usually have stuff going on after school, so I need it then.

Ms. Busymom: All right, that's four nights. We'll note that down here Tuesday, Thursday, Friday, and Saturday. Now, Sally, what about you?

Sally: Mom, this is completely unfair! I need the car on Friday or Saturday if I'm going to have any life at all!

Ms. Busymom: Let's not get into "fair" and "unfair," honey. We'll work out a fair arrangement for you both. Right now we just need to get the facts down on paper. Which nights do you need the car?

Sally: Friday and Saturday nights for sure. And Tuesdays and Sundays I'm going to be volunteering at the nursing home and I need a way to get there. Wednesday I've got band practice after school, and since you work late on Wednesdays and can't pick me up, I need to have the car then.

Ms. Busymom: Okay, let's see what we have here. Nobody needs the car on Monday; on Tuesday you both need it; Wednesday, just Sally needs it; Thursday, Bob, you need it; Friday and Saturday you both want it; and Sunday Sally has to have it. Is that right?

Bob: Yeah.

Ms. Busymom: So the problem days are Tuesdays, Fridays, and Saturdays. Now Tuesday, Bob, you can drop your sister off at the nursing home on your way to Gloria's house, and you can pick her up at nine when she gets off.

Bob: But what if we want to study later?

Ms. Busymom: You're going to have to stick to nine as your cutoff time if you want to use the car on Tuesday. This is a contract, remember? You can't get something without giving something.

Bob: Okay, but just make sure you're ready to leave at nine.

Sally: You just make sure you're there when I'm ready to go. I don't want to stand in the rain waiting while you and Gloria . . .

Bob: Okay, what's next, Mom? What about the weekend? I *have* to have the car on the weekends.

Ms. Busymom: So does your sister. And I assume you don't want to spend your Friday and Saturday evenings together.

Bob and Sally: No!

Ms. Busymom: So there are a couple of ways we can work this out. The easiest one is just to alternate. Bob gets the car every Friday night, and Sally, you get the car every Saturday.

Sally: But Mom, suppose I've got something going on Friday night?

Ms. Busymom: Well, you have a choice: You can arrange an alternate means of transportation, or we can make an arrangement where you and your brother switch days every week. Bob gets the car on Friday one weekend and on Saturday the next. Of course, that means you'll have to plan your activities a bit in advance, but that shouldn't be a huge problem. Anyway, some planning might be good for the two of you.

Bob: I guess we could do something like that. I'd rather switch nights back and forth. That way I'm not just tied to Friday nights.

Sally: Okay, I guess we can do that.

Ms. Busymom: All right, based on what you two have agreed to, I'm going to draw up the contract, and you'll both sign it. But I'm going to add a rider.

Bob: What's that?

Ms. Busyman: It's an additional clause that says that this arrangement depends on both of you maintaining at least a B average at school. If you fall below that, the contact is null and void, and the other person gets exclusive use of the car. If you both drop below a B, we put the car in the garage and neither of you gets to use it. Are we clear on that?

Sally: Yes. What happens if we get our grades back up to a B again?

Ms. Busyman: Then the terms of the contract kick in and we go back to this arrangement. Also, either of you can ask for a renegotiation of the contract at any time, but it will be settled in a negotiating session like this one. Okay?

Sally and Bob: Okay, Mom.

If only all teenage disputes could be settled so easily. Take notice of a few things that happened here:

1. Both children are now held to a specific agreement with defined rules, so there are no more gray areas. The more clearly you set out the terms of your agreement with your children, the less room there is for disputes later on.

2. Bob and Sally learned the important lesson that in any negotiation *you have to give up something to get something*. With luck, this will make future negotiations with them easier.

3. Because Ms. Busymom has been able to serve as impartial arbiter between her two offspring, she's able to impose her own conditions on the deal. She's used the car as an incentive for both children to keep their grades at an acceptable level.

Chapter 11

Great
Negotiations

WHETHER YOU'RE EMBARKING ON a career path filled with negotiations or trying to get through a single life-changing event, the basics you've learned from this book—and the skills you'll develop through practice—will remain with you forever. Keep your knowledge fresh and your skills sharp by accessing them often, and be willing to learn from every experience. In this chapter, you'll learn the key strategies that the world's most successful negotiators use every day. Try them on and see how they fit. Over time, you'll recognize what brings you the most success.

Establish Trust

Before you find yourself in your counterparts' good graces, you must first give them the opportunity to trust you. Once they feel like you're trustworthy, that's it—you're in. Rapport develops more naturally because you've proven that you're not just "in it to win it," you're in it to develop solutions that work. This level of trust can be accomplished by fostering your negotiating relationships every step of the way. **Once you've established that trust, it's important to maintain it.**

The best way to gain your counterpart's trust is with actions that demonstrate your reliability and commitment. Just saying "You can trust me" or "I'm an honest person" won't sound very convincing. Worse, some may assume that just the opposite is true. You want the other party to pick up on your sincerity, and this can't happen if you come off too strong by being too eager to make a good impression. Consequently, it will be more difficult for you to work on the relationship if the other person is skeptical about what you say.

▶ Set the Tone

You want the other party to feel comfortable working with you right from the beginning. One way to accomplish this is to be clear that you would like to approach the discussion by brainstorming to find the most effective solutions for both of you. Explain that you feel both of you have much more to gain by working together instead of against each other. If the other party agrees, be sure to show your **enthusiasm**. If you get resistance, ask for a description of the other party's main goal, and provide the reasons that your approach is the best way to reach it. Because you're not being demanding about how you'd like to conduct the discussion, the other party will surely note your cooperative skills and optimistic outlook.

ENTHUSIASM: You know this when you see it; it's excitement or passion about a given topic. Enthusiasm is contagious. If you show how much you care about the negotiation you're taking part in, the other party will likely be inspired to do the same.

How you present yourself can make all the difference when you enter the negotiation room. The way you carry yourself says a lot to your counterpart about the attitude you're taking toward the discussion and toward him. When you first see him, present a genuine smile, a firm handshake, and say something nice, like "How was your flight?" or "It's good to see you again."

The atmosphere you create can influence your counterpart in deciding whether to trust you. If you break the ice by being the first one to talk, you'll have the advantage of setting a positive tone. Being in the driver's seat also allows you to get to know the other party a little better because you're in a position to be the first to ask questions. Furthermore, you can direct the conversation and get the agenda underway by asking questions related to specific topics.

▶ Be Approachable

No matter how much knowledge or leverage you have, throwing your weight around will only succeed in distancing your counterpart. Instead, relate to her by showing you are just as much a human being as she is. Express your feelings about any issue or possible outcome you don't agree with, but be sure to stay in control of your emotions, remaining calm and collected. Talk about why something doesn't work for you, and look for common elements that will help you come up with a solution that does. Portraying a positive attitude shows the other party that you're willing to look at problems from every angle in order to get to the bottom of them.

The more you show your counterparts your honest side, the more they'll trust you. Of course, you don't want to give everything away and make yourself a target, but you do want to let them know where you're coming from so they're aware of the challenges you have to face. Giving away this bit of information is also a time-saver because you're able to work around the roadblocks and resolve differences more quickly.

A positive viewpoint is another element that shows how easy you are to talk to and work with. If you want the other party to let his guard down a little, you'll have to do the same. Laughter is a great way to lighten up the mood in any situation, and it also gets people talking again. If you're stuck on an issue and you both feel you've exhausted every possible angle, find a way to joke about it. You'll instantly begin to loosen up and hopefully be able to move on with the topic you're discussing. Don't be afraid to get dramatic! Stand up, walk over to the window, and say something like, "Aha! The answer to our problem lies somewhere out there in that busy street. Now if only we can find it." This little tension breaker might be all you need to put you back on that road to discovery.

▶ Do What You Say You'll Do

When people say they'll get back to you, isn't it nice when they actually do? A person who lives up to his obligation is the first person you contact for information, even if several other people can easily provide you with it.

Dependable people are incredibly valuable. If your counterpart did not fulfill an obligation to the shipping company, you will have to delay the shipment of products to your customers, making them angry and possibly distrustful of your company's practices. Similarly, you'll begin to distrust your counterpart because of that failure to come through on an acknowledged duty.

Avoid making promises you aren't sure you can keep. If someone asks you a question that you can't answer, say that you'll look into the issue—and really mean it. Each time you make good on a promise, whether big or small, it will be remembered. The more you live up to your end of the deal, the more good things you say about your character.

Build Relationships

As you now know, the relationships you build during the negotiation process aren't the same as the ones you have with your parents or children or friends. They're business relationships, and they come with a list of **caveats**. For instance, you must beware of a rushed timeline, or be careful not to give up too much information too quickly. But like any other, these relationships are built on trust, respect, and mutual interest. Negotiations will always go more smoothly if both parties have a positive experience.

CAVEAT: A caveat is a warning or caution. Some caveats are serious, such as when a colleague warns you about a client's aggressive negotiating style. Others are mild but still important to keep in mind, such as a real-estate agent's tendency to communicate via e-mail instead of the phone.

Think about the relationship you're trying to build with your counterpart. How can you continue to improve it so you both leave the negotiation feeling a sense of partnership? The answer lies in how open you're willing to be. While you never want to lay all your cards out on the table, it is important that you give the other party new information if the situation calls for it. This allows her to see your point more clearly, and it gives her the opportunity to respond with an equal amount of openness. The result? You both learn something fundamental about each other's role in the deal.

▶ Have an Open Mind

When we find a system that works, we tend to use it over and over again. Similarly, when we find a negotiating style we're comfortable with, we use it every chance we get. But all successful negotiators know how important it is to tailor their style to match the other party's behavior. If your style involves analyzing every detail and your counterpart's is to be more direct, it's a good idea to summarize your findings rather than discussing every element. If you and the other party are equally skilled negotiators, you will both be making the same effort to adapt to each other's needs.

As long as you remember that all negotiators have their own way of doing things and nobody is right or wrong, then you can make it in any negotiation. The importance of being open-minded is especially apparent during the bargaining phase, in which everyone tries to find the best way to reach agreements. When the negotiation reaches that point, be respectful to everyone's ideas, and seriously think about each one. **Be honest about whether you think something works, and give explanations for why you feel the way you do.**

▶ Create an Atmosphere of Respect

Successful negotiators understand the importance of working in an atmosphere that's comfortable and conflict-free. They also know that while some level of stress is to be expected, creating more stress on top of that is unnecessary. For this reason, they don't behave irrationally by insulting the other party, and they use their best listening skills. Additionally, they are firm on the issues that are important to them while remaining calm and unemotional.

A negotiator of this caliber knows that if you are a professional, you need to act like one. They instinctively know what the other party is thinking, and just to be sure, they ask questions that show their willingness to learn more about the other party's objectives. Just thinking about negotiating in this kind of atmosphere is enough to produce a calm effect!

By now, you must be wondering how these exceptional negotiators learned to be so proficient at what they do. Among their many skills, one of the most important is that they understand human nature. They know that some people can't control their emotions when faced with tough decisions; that people change their minds on a **whim**; that it's in our genes to become aggressive when we're not getting our way. Throughout all of these challenges, the successful negotiator never loses her cool, never takes it personally, and never stops pushing to reach a jointly designed win-win outcome.

WHIM: A whim is a sudden desire. When someone does or says something "on a whim" they are doing it spontaneously, without thinking it through. The middle of a negotiation is no time to act on a whim, but that doesn't mean you or your counterpart won't do it from time to time!

▶ Handle Power Appropriately

Power itself is not a negative thing to possess; rather, it's how people sometimes misuse power that gives it a bad reputation. Using it to control other people is unethical and one-sided, while using it to produce a positive result is productive. Sometimes people have the power to make changes, but they don't use it because they're either unaware that they have it or they just don't make the effort.

Though some negotiators believe that there is always one person who has more power than the other, the opposite is actually true. If someone did hold all the power, why would they need the other person to help them achieve their goals? In fact, you should never underestimate how strong the other party actually is, because their strength may show up in unexpected ways.

▶ Play Fair

In order for you as a negotiator to set the stage for success and gain respect from your counterpart, you must **use win-win negotiation strategies every step of the way**. When people enter into a negotiation, they expect to be treated as if their needs were not that important. What they don't expect is the very thing that you should give them—star treatment. When you demonstrate that your counterpart's needs are important to the success of your goals, you'll gain immediate respect.

Stick to your goals, but be kind about it. Question ideas, but don't criticize. Be yourself, but be considerate of your counterpart's personality. Keep discussions moving forward, but don't rush through the issues. Encourage new ideas, but take them seriously. Every successful negotiator knows that ruthlessness will get you nowhere fast.

"See" the Deal

The ability to dream is a powerful tool in all aspects of life. When it comes to negotiating, it's something that allows you to discover many possibilities. If you envision how the meeting will unfold, you can better prepare for potential situations. If you let your imagination run wild, you can think up all sorts of scenarios and plan how to handle them if they take place. Sparking the creative side of your brain even before the preparation stage gives you the opportunity to get ready for the unexpected by developing a myriad of protective strategies. For instance, if you concoct a hypothetical situation in which your counterpart suddenly brings more team members into the negotiation, you can then put together a plan for countering that move.

This **preemptive** step can end up saving you a lot of time because the solutions you think up can also be used to resolve disputes you're having in other areas of the discussion.

Another way to use your imagination for planning purposes is to come up with probable outcomes of all your and the other party's possible issues. This will help you establish your settlement range because you'll be able to place a level of importance on each possible outcome. It will also help you direct the negotiation toward solution-oriented discussions instead of getting stuck on one issue after another.

PREEMPTIVE: A preemptive act is an anticipatory one; you're trying to prepare for something you expect to happen. For instance, if you think your opponent might offer a discount if you promise to buy a year's supply of their product, make your move first in the hope of encouraging them to make theirs.

▶ Predict Variables

In order to conduct a thorough analysis of the negotiation, take it apart to investigate each of its parts, and then see how many ways you can put it back together. Experiment with the parts by seeing if and how they relate to each other. For example, can you offer the other party a lower shipping fee and make up for it in the cost of installation? Out of all the financial issues, is any one interchangeable and if so, how flexible can you afford to be? How strict are certain deadlines compared to others, and can they be extended? The answers to these questions will provide you with a good overview of what you gain and what you stand to lose with each issue.

You can also use the process as an aid in determining the importance of individual issues. Prioritizing is essential because you'll need to know when you should pick your battles and when you shouldn't. An issue of great importance should never be compromised, and you should be as firm as possible without being demanding. Let the other party know that you cannot bend on certain issues, but also offer a few different suggestions that benefit him as well.

Additionally, back up your position with tangible evidence, such as printed reports or company documents. This lets the other party see firsthand how serious the issue is. It also might encourage him to do the same for you when the time comes.

▶ Prepare for Change

Since the act of negotiation doesn't follow a set pattern, something is inevitably going to change, and you need to be prepared for it. This change could be in the other party's behavior at closing. For example, she suddenly wants to take back most of her concessions because she's having second thoughts. It will then be up to you to point out how she's benefiting from the agreements that were made and why the negotiation should move forward.

Another way change occurs is when a solution you thought was workable suddenly becomes unacceptable because of other agreements that were made. If this happens, you'll have to look at the agreements affecting the change, determine which one is more important, and discuss how it can be reworked to find the best solution. For example, while you're discussing your need to have at least 40 percent of the shipping costs paid for, the other party discovers that the high price agreed upon to pay for installation will make the cost for shipping prohibitive. Clearly, both issues need to be re-evaluated to determine how the costs can be adjusted.

You'll lose a little time because you'll have to go back and renegotiate something that was already settled. However, it's a good idea to reassess your goals because you might feel differently about their priority levels as the discussion moves along.

▶ Have a Walk-Away Point

One of the most important things you can bring with you to the table is your walk-away point. Without this, you can negotiate for hours, giving everything away without getting any of your needs met.

Having a walk-away point gives you leverage; without you, there's no way for the other party to realize any goals. However, use it only when absolutely necessary or else you risk losing the opportunity to devise a mutual solution. Give your counterpart the chance to work with you, and make it clear that you don't want to walk away if you don't have to.

It's All about Communication

If you think about it, we should all be experts on communication—we have so many ways of doing it, from the telephone to e-mail. However, when we get together to discuss big issues face to face, some of us have a hard time conveying the right things at the right time. The only way to get better at communication is to practice it and take notice of what works and what doesn't. Even if you don't recognize your mistakes, your counterpart will probably point them out for you.

▶ Self-Confidence Is Key

Master negotiators are comfortable no matter where they negotiate, what they negotiate, or whom they negotiate with. They know that in order to get their message across, they have to be confident enough to make enthusiastic presentations about their ideas as well as argue their needs with the use of well-prepared facts. Every interaction they have with a counterpart has a purpose, whether it's to convey an idea, discuss an issue, examine a possible solution, or learn something.

They also know screaming and threatening does not make things any better. The only purpose this type of interaction serves is to instill fear in the other person, at which point the exchange of information and ideas is cut off altogether. The successful negotiator knows that the best way to be firm about something is to use tone of voice and a careful choice of words to illustrate a point.

▶ **Be an Active Listener**

Part of what helps you develop excellent communication skills is having excellent listening skills. This requires more than just hearing what's coming out of the other party's mouth. Actively participate in absorbing the information you're given. Nod your head in agreement to important points, and write down questions that you want to ask when the presentation is finished.

Let the other party have the floor without interruption. This technique is a good relationship builder because it shows you're genuinely interested in learning. Take notes so you can ask for explanations of anything you didn't understand, and express your eagerness about some of the ideas.

Never Sell Yourself Short

In order to get what you want, you need to ask for it. As obvious as that concept may seem, it's easy to forget when you're trying to build your strategy. You might be too intimidated to ask for more than what you really need because you don't want to offend the other party and risk losing something important. Skilled negotiators are never afraid to ask for something, even if they already have a mile-long wish list. They know that it never hurts to ask and that it's better to get a bunch of negative responses than to wonder later about whether you could have gotten what you didn't ask for.

If you're still worried that you might be asking for more than you should, make a separate list of concessions that you can offer in case the other party gets frustrated with all your requests. Think of concessions that won't hurt that much to give up but that might mean a lot from the receiving end.

Your **aspirations** determine how satisfied you will be with the outcome of the negotiation. Even if a win-win resolution has been achieved, there's still the possibility of feeling like you didn't get quite what you wanted. The reason for this is that you didn't set your goals high enough, possibly because you felt you were being fair to the other party and saving face in the relationship. A good negotiator realizes that it's a lot tougher to upgrade a goal that was set too low once it's out in the open than it is to lower a goal that started off high. The same holds true if you're a seller and you don't set the price high enough in the beginning. While you want to set a reasonable price, you also want to give yourself enough room to counter the other party's offer.

ASPIRATION: An aspiration is a goal or objective. You should always have your goals clearly defined before you enter into a negotiation, and have in mind which ones you absolutely must have and which you're willing to give up.

It's important to have confidence in your goals and to set a bottom line for each one. **Know exactly what you want and how far you're willing to go to get it**, and you can't get taken advantage of. Use research as your most powerful tool when determining price, especially for big-ticket items such as a car or house. Doing so will give you even more confidence because you can justify your bottom line with tangible proof.

A Learning Experience

Occasionally, a negotiation will "fail." The other party will achieve their goals while you make concessions you had hoped not to make, or you'll lose the deal altogether to a competitor. Don't beat yourself up; instead, take advantage of the opportunity you've been given. Recognizing and studying these failures will help you identify which areas need improvement and which ones are working well. Because experience is the best teacher, **it takes time, patience, and perseverance to acquire and develop the skills needed to become a successful negotiator**.

▶ Inadequate Preparation

If you don't make the effort to adequately prepare for every step of the negotiation process, you're least likely to achieve a satisfactory outcome. This is the first and most crucial phase in the process. Each one of your arguments will be based on the information you turn up during your research. Even if you spend weeks doing research, you must have the right information, or you risk being caught off guard by the other party. Here are a few knowledge gaps that are evidence of poor planning:

- Lack of information
- No plan for an opening
- No bottom line
- Inaccurate facts
- Poor or no organization skills
- Unorganized agenda
- Vague in the details (dates, prices, quantities)
- Not enough information about the other party

To be sure you're prepared, make a list of the points you need to research. Since this step is the most important one, make sure you give yourself plenty of time. Double-check factual information, and find the answers to every question you have.

▶ Poor Communication

Negotiating is all about exchanging ideas and interacting with the other party. When something inhibits the process, it's very difficult to find solutions to the problems you're facing. If you and the other party don't seem to be communicating in a way that's beneficial to the discussion, the best thing you can do to clear the air is to say, "I don't feel like we're communicating very well." Work together to pinpoint the problem before you go any further. The following list will help you recognize some of these problems:

- A level of trust hasn't been established.
- One person is dominating every conversation.
- The other party does not have authority to make decisions.
- Disagreements are taken too personally.

- Creative thinking, brainstorming, and problem-solving are not taking place.
- Body language is not being observed.
- No one is asking questions.
- Only one side is making concessions.
- Irrational, hostile, and/or abusive behavior is displayed.
- The other party does not know how to negotiate.
- Someone has a negative outlook.

Any kind of mistreatment will hinder the injured party's desire to communicate. Respect and trust are two of the most important factors in conducting a professional discussion. Without them, suspicion remains constant throughout the negotiation, and you will never feel comfortable with what the other party is saying.

▶ Too Many Mistakes

It's true what they say: Everyone makes mistakes. Furthermore, it's necessary that we make these mistakes so we can learn from the consequences they produce and avoid making them next time. Even if you feel you didn't make any mistakes with a particular negotiation, look for mistakes your counterpart might have made and learn from those. The following are some of the most common oversights:

- Acceptance of the first offer
- Lack of focus
- Inability to adapt to other person's style
- Inflexibility
- Forgetting about one's goals
- Becoming too emotional

Take your time, and make sure you feel comfortable about every decision that's made before moving on to the next issue. Keep moving toward the close, and be attentive to the other party's objectives as well as your own.

Enjoy the Ride

When you first picked up this book, you might have been dreading the experience of learning how to negotiate. True, it can have its awkward and frustrating moments, but a good negotiation will leave you surprised at how much enjoyment you receive from it. Not only do you get the opportunity to achieve your goals, you get to work with (and learn from) some very talented and skilled people. Together, you and your counterpart embark on a journey of discovery and creativity in which the perfect plan is developed. Along the way, you engage in thought-provoking discussions that invigorate the mind and refresh the pool of ideas that you've amassed. As a result, the bonds you form help lead to agreements and further the possibility of future commitments.

You've done the hard work of studying the strategies and learning what to say; now it's time to go out there and have some fun! Like anything in life, your negotiating experience will be more rewarding if you remember that it's not only about the destination, it's also about the journey. So get down to business—and enjoy the ride!

Key Words in This Chapter
- Enthusiasm
- Caveat
- Whim
- Preemptive
- Aspiration

Key Phrases in This Chapter
- Once you've established that trust, it's important to maintain it.
- The more you show your counterparts your honest side, the more they'll trust you.
- Dependable people are incredibly valuable.
- Be honest about whether you think something works, and give explanations for why you feel the way you do.

- Use win-win negotiation strategies every step of the way.
- One of the most important things you can bring with you to the table is your walk-away point.
- Let the other party have the floor without interruption.
- In order to get what you want, you need to ask for it.
- Know exactly what you want and how far you're willing to go to get it.
- It takes time, patience, and perseverance to acquire and develop the skills needed to become a successful negotiator.

Case Study—Negotiate with Confidence

Let's take a look at one final scenario that sums up what we've discussed in this book. Ms. Salesexec is working out a deal with Mr. Superstore regarding the delivery of product during the Christmas holidays. Watch the back-and-forth flow of the discussion between them to see how they overcome obstacles.

Ms. Salesexec: So what we have to decide is the schedule on which we can make September deliveries, right?

Mr. Superstore: Yes. This is going to be tricky, because we've got a lot of sales going on over the Christmas holidays, and we need to have all the merchandise in the warehouse by the beginning of October.

Ms. Salesexec: But then you're increasing your warehousing costs by having to store the product for three months. Couldn't you take delivery a month later? That would ease things for us on the production end.

Mr. Superstore: Well . . .

Ms. Salesexec: Please let me know if this doesn't work for you. I think it's important that we be completely honest here. If an arrangement doesn't work, it's not going to benefit either one of us.

Mr. Superstore: The thing is that we've scheduled to take on extra staff at the warehouse in October. We estimate that with our new computer systems and fulfillment systems, it'll take us a month or so to get everything fully up and running, and we want your product in the warehouse to make sure our people know how to handle it. We've got to give them a little time to find their feet.

Ms. Salesexec: I understand where you're coming from. What concerns me is that to meet the earlier deadline we'd have to add staff to our production facilities, and that would push the price per unit up.

Mr. Superstore: To what?

Ms. Salesexec: I'll have to double-check with our people, of course, but I think we could be looking at a per-unit increase of ten to fifteen cents.

Mr. Superstore: That's quite a bit. Are you sure it would be that much?

Ms. Salesexec: Not entirely. As I say, I'll have to go back and crunch some numbers with the production folks. But the fact is that what you're proposing is a very early date for us, and I just don't know if we can make it.

Mr. Superstore: What kind of flexibility do you have on that?

Ms. Salesexec: I really don't have any, to be honest. These numbers are going to be what they are, and I'm afraid you'll just have to take my word on this. However, let's see if we can find another solution to the problem. Do you need the full order delivery in September?

Mr. Superstore: We could probably look at a partial delivery. How much did you have in mind?

Ms. Salesexec: Well, assuming that we keep our staff at its current levels, I'd say we could fulfill approximately 50 percent of the order by the beginning of September. That would give your staff something to work with, and by the time they went through that amount of product, we could deliver another 25 percent of the order by the first of October and the final 25 percent by mid-October.

Mr. Superstore: That would probably work, but it might create some pacing problems for us. Would you be supplying all the parts that we'd need to ship or would the order come in with just one kind of part followed by another?

Ms. Salesexec: What would work better for you?

Mr. Superstore: Obviously we'd prefer to be able to start shipping to our outlets as soon as possible, given our schedule, so I'd rather have a partial order from you that contains everything we need to begin that shipping process.

Ms. Salesexec: I think that can happen, but this will mean retooling some of our production process, so again you're going to be looking at a price increase.

Mr. Superstore: How much for this one?

Ms. Salesexec: With the caveats I told you before, I've got to crunch these numbers and run them by Production and Finance. I think we could probably do this for a per-unit cost of five cents.

Mr. Superstore: Well, that's a lot better than ten to fifteen cents.

Ms. Salesexec: Much better. Do you think this arrangement could work?

Mr. Superstore: I think so. It sounds as if what we need is a clear, firm delivery schedule and a chance to prepare everyone on our teams to meet it. I'd like to see the contract include as an appendix a guaranteed schedule with specifications as to penalties for not meeting it, since I have to be able to assure everyone on my team that we're protected financially if something goes wrong on the production end.

Ms. Salesexec: I don't see that as a problem. When I have our legal people draft the contract, I'll have them put together that schedule, and you and I can go over the details when we review the contract.

Mr. Superstore: Great! Ms. Salesexec, good doing business with you.

Ms. Salesexec: And with you, Mr. Superstore.

As this chapter has pointed out, negotiations work best when both sides are honest with each other and specify precisely what they want and why they need it. In this instance:

1. Mr. Superstore explained the problem on his end to Ms. Salesexec and told her what his overall goal was. The result was that she was able to propose a solution that worked for him.

2. Each party in the discussion was respectful of the other's viewpoint and didn't interrupt or badger—both of these are no-nos in negotiation, though as explained in an earlier chapter you may encounter these as tactics employed by an Intimidator.

3. Both sides were willing to give in order to get—the essence of win-win negotiation techniques. As a result, Mr. Superstore and Ms. Salesexec will both probably have good holiday seasons, and their two companies will continue to maintain a productive working relationship with one another.

Appendix A

Quick-
Reference
Checklists

This section contains some of the major points that were covered in this book, compiled into convenient checklists that you can easily review any time you need to. They also come in handy if you want to make sure you've covered all your bases before entering into a negotiation. If it helps, make a copy of the pages and keep them with you throughout the entire process so you always have a quick reference guide by your side.

Before You Negotiate
- Define your main goal.
- Prioritize the rest of your goals.
- Decide on the concessions you're willing to make.
- Define your bottom line.
- Research your counterpart.
- Highlight your common goals, and note differences.
- Gather as much information as possible.
- Have alternatives.
- Devise a strategy for a win-win outcome.
- Create an agenda.
- Choose a meeting spot.

While You Negotiate
- Compare your agenda with the other party's agenda.
- Agree on conducting a win-win discussion.
- Listen attentively to your counterpart's needs.
- Verify that the other party has authority to make decisions.
- Bargain concession for concession.
- Pay attention to body language.
- Brainstorm to find the best solution.
- Make your bottom line known at the right time.
- Reveal that you have alternatives.
- Make decisions that move toward closing.

Ending the Negotiation

- Take a break before closing.
- Review and confirm every agreement.
- Avoid making and agreeing to last-minute concessions.
- Encourage your counterpart to end the deal.
- Point out the benefits of each agreement.
- Read the contract carefully.
- Ask questions about anything you don't understand.
- Initial and date changes that are made to the contract.
- Make a list of deadline concessions to follow up on.

Appendix B

Glossary

Add-on
A small concession that a party asks for by adding it to a larger concession that's already been discussed.

Alternative dispute resolution
A process that includes either mediation or arbitration that parties use to avoid a lawsuit.

Arbitration
A type of alternative dispute resolution that involves the intervention of a third party, an arbitrator. The arbitrator directs a hearing and decides who gets what.

Bad faith
When a party makes concessions with no intention of fulfilling them.

Bargaining
Discussing the terms of a sale until an agreement is made.

Barter
An exchange of goods or services without the use of money.

Body language
Nonverbal cues that give some indication about what a party is really thinking.

Boilerplate or form contract
A template that some companies use as their basic contract for every client; lists the conditions and limitations of the agreement.

Bottom line
The point in which the deal is no longer negotiable; your walk-away point.

Breach of contract
When a party does something that goes against a signed contract; failing to perform duties; refusing to do what's expected.

Concession
A privilege that's given to the other party in exchange for something else.

Consequential and incidental damages
Money awarded by the court to the injured party for losses that were predicted if a breach of contract occurred.

Consideration
A term for benefits, gains, promises, or services rendered.

Delay tactic
A tactic that is used to stall a negotiation or to gain more time than is probably needed.

Devil's advocate
A training technique in which a person tests your arguments by systematically rejecting everything you offer so you can see all the possible things that could go wrong.

Failure of consideration
When a party does not hold up to its agreed part of the contract.

Good faith
The implication that everyone will be fair and truthful in order to satisfy the purpose of the negotiation.

Good guy/bad guy tactic

An act in which one person pretends to be difficult, aggressive, and unyielding, while another person on the same negotiating team pretends to be on your side.

Imaginary deadline

A proposed deadline that is not real; usually invoked to gain more time.

Leverage

Something (information, experience, options) that gives a party more of an advantage.

Low-balling

A tactic in which an offer lower than the norm is made.

Market conditions

The current climate for making a certain type of purchase or other negotiation. When buying a house, for instance, market conditions include determining whether you're in a seller's or buyer's market (supply vs. demand), whether interest rates are high or low, and what the home sale trends are.

Market value

The price you can expect for the item you hope to buy or sell. In the case of real estate, often determined by what other houses sold for in the neighborhood you're looking to buy in.

Mediation

A type of alternative dispute resolution that involves the intervention of a third party—a mediator—to help parties resolve issues.

Nibbling
When a party asks for "one more thing" after an agreement has already been reached.

One-time only offer
A high-pressure tactic in which a party will pretend that an offer is only good for that day.

Positional or win-lose negotiating
One party reaches desired goals at the expense of the other party.

Release
When a party relinquishes claims, actions, and/or any rights against another party, freeing them of any responsibilities that were stated in an agreement.

Settlement range
The spectrum of possible outcomes between your ideal and worst-case scenarios.

Stress
The emphasis that is placed on words; one of the elements that make up tone.

Win-win negotiating
Both parties work together to achieve an outcome that is fair and mutually satisfying.

Appendix C

Resources

You've got the basics down, but if you want to continue educating yourself about particular aspects of negotiating, there's a lot of information available to you. This appendix includes suggestions for books and websites that may be beneficial to beginning negotiators.

▶ Further Reading

Brodow, Ed. *Negotiation Boot Camp: How to Resolve Conflict, Satisfy Customers, and Make Better Deals* (Currency Doubleday: 2006).

Burrell, Tim. *Create a Great Deal: The Art of Real Estate Negotiating* (The Silloway Press: 2009).

Dawson, Roger. *Secrets of Power Negotiating: Inside Secrets from a Master Negotiator* (Career Press: 2011).

Diamond, Stuart. *Getting More: How to Negotiate to Achieve Your Goals in the Real World* (Crown Business: 2010).

Fisher, Roger and William Ury. *Getting to Yes: Negotiating Agreement Without Giving In* (Penguin Books: 2011).

Ford, Bob. *What Car Dealers Won't Tell You: The Insider's Guide to Buying or Leasing a New or Used Car* (Plume: 2005).

Malhotra, Deepak and Max H. Bazerman. *Negotiation Genius: How to Overcome Obstacles and Achieve Brilliant Results at the Bargaining Table and Beyond* (Bantam Dell: 2008).

Margulies, Sam, PhD, JD. *Getting Divorced Without Ruining Your Life* (Simon & Schuster: 2001).

Miller, Lee E. and Jessica. *A Woman's Guide to Successful Negotiating: How to Convince, Collaborate, and Create Your Way to Agreement* (McGraw-Hill: 2011).

Ordway, Nicholas. *The Absolute Beginner's Guide to Buying a House* (Prima Publishing: 2002).

Shell, G. Richard. *Bargaining for Advantage: Negotiating Strategies for Reasonable People* (Penguin Books: 2006).

▶ **Websites**

Advanced Public Speaking Institute: *www.public-speaking.org* contains hundreds of articles on the subject of negotiation

Entrepreneur: *www.entrepreneur.com* Covers a variety of business topics and allows you to conduct a search for articles on negotiating

Everyone Negotiates: *www.everyonenegotiates.com* is a great resource for learning and sharpening skills

FindLaw: *www.findlaw.com* is a site to find a lawyer in your city, printable forms, product recalls, and more

Free Advice: *www.freeadvice.com* offers legal advice on a variety of topics

JobStar Central: *www.jobstar.org* is a job search guide with tons of articles on negotiating salary

Legaldocs: *www.legaldocs.com* provides printable legal documents

Nolo: *www.nolo.com* explains the law in terms the rest of us can understand

Roger Dawson's Power Negotiating Institute: *www.rdawson* *.com* is one of the industry's leading business speakers and authors

SalaryExpert: *www.salaryexpert.com* offers individual and executive salary reports

▶ Negotiation Workshops

Dr. Chester L. Karass Negotiation Skill Training Program: *www.karrass.com*

Negotiations Training Institute: *www.negotiationsworkshops.com* details a number of negotiation workshops

Sales Training America: *www.salestrainingamerica.com*

Index

Note: Page numbers in **bold** indicate definitions/primary use of key negotiation terms. Page numbers in *italics* indicate key phrase information.